To   3/17/23

With [joy?] that God brought you into The St. Timothy's "orbit!"

Blessings,
Chris

CRAZY GOD STUFF

TWELVE LESSONS I LEARNED BEFORE DYING

CHRIS SCHULLER

Copyright © 2018 by Chris Schuller

All rights reserved. This book or any portion thereof may not be reproduced or used in any manner whatsoever without the express written permission of the publisher except for the use of brief quotations in a book review.

Printed in the United States of America

First Printing, 2018

For my sister Constance Faith, whose faith in me, however unmerited, has truly been a constant in my life.

Table of Contents

Preface i

Eric Waddell and Mark Washington 1

Nuclear Obsession 11

Adrenal Gland 17

Born to Fly: Bruce Springsteen & the AMC Pacer   29

Kim & The Ouija Board 37

Abortion Healing 45

Jesus' Birthday 51

Carole Gerbracht Dies 57

Carole Gerbracht's Funeral 67

Carole Victorious 77

Overprotective 91

Meeting Mister President 103

PREFACE

Crazy God Stuff is a collection of stories, all true, which for most of my life I've kept to myself. Of course I've shared some of them with friends, but I kept several of them almost entirely to myself for fear that if I did share them with people, they'd think that I was crazy and that the events hadn't actually happened.

That all changed last year when I was in a serious auto accident, died, and was miraculously resuscitated. An unexpected benefit of the crash was this: When I came back to life, my fears stayed dead. Whatever worries I once had about sharing my deepest truths disappeared, as did all of my other fears.

I mention the car wreck also as an explanation of the second half of the book's title, "Twelve Lessons I Learned before Dying." To be truthful, my pulse never stopped, but at 14 beats per minute with a blood pressure of 40/20, I took complete leave of my body for most of a day and a half. When my soul (or spirit, if you prefer) was reunited with my body for good, I felt like I had been re-born, which was serendipitous, since it happened on March 12th, my actual birthday.

And there is some form of serendipity, or even outright miracle, in every one of these stories. As an example of that, I actually believe that I know Jesus' birthdate (He's a Libra, not a Capricorn). But more amazing than learning the date was the way it was revealed to me, and by whom.

I know from public readings of the chapter Jesus' Birthday that everyone in the group felt a similar rush of wonder and awe at God's grace and generosity.

The ways I've experienced that divine grace and generosity have varied enormously depending on my circumstances or seasons of life. Even before my car accident, I'd had a few close calls with death and, in one case, learned that God's actions are not bound by the laws of physics. The full story is in the chapter, Born to Fly: Bruce Springsteen and the AMC Pacer.

I hope this book gives you joy, but even more, I hope it inspires you to have the courage to share your own most miraculous moments with others, no matter how crazy they might sound!

- Chris Schuller

Eric Waddell
&
Mark Washington

In 1967, my family moved from Webster Groves, one of the wealthiest suburbs in St. Louis, Missouri, to a part of Dayton, Ohio, called Dayton View. My father, a Lutheran seminary professor and author, had created a bit of a name for himself as an expert on "urban ministry" which was code for ministry to people who were usually black and always poor — and wanted his kids to experience something different than the white Protestant wealth of Webster Groves. Between my dad's urban agenda, and the fact that we could buy an aging mansion for half of what the same house cost in Oakwood (Dayton's W.A.S.P-y equivalent to Webster Groves), Dayton View was the clear choice.

Thinking back on it, it's almost a miracle how incredibly diverse that neighborhood was in 1967. It had a blend of blacks, whites and Jews, and although I didn't know what gay people were, I did know that a few homes had adult men in them who weren't brothers. In addition, there was economic diversity, ranging from the millionaire lawyer across the street to the man three doors down who worked the line at the Huffy bike factory.

This diversity was more transitional than intentional, however, and real estate agents would regularly call our house (not knowing we'd just moved into the neighborhood) to suggest that we should sell and move out before "negroes lower your property value." This racist fear-mongering, called block-busting, had a self-fulfilling component. By 1970 my fifth grade class at my local public elementary school, Cornell Heights, was 90% black and 10% white, and few, if any, of that white minority were Jewish.

It was at Cornell Heights that I learned to be as black as a white person can be, which, by virtue of my skin remaining white, is not at all. But I did draw pictures of soul singers, African-American profiles with huge Afro hairdo's, and then I'd write underneath my drawings "SOUL BROTHER # 1" or, more precisely, "JAMES BROWN." We boys were more likely to draw pictures of Mr. Brown, while the girls drew pictures of Aretha Franklin, "SOUL SISTER #1."

Although I drew pictures of James Brown and Aretha, and could sing along in my high pre-adolescent voice to R-E-S-P-E-C-T and even "Chain of Fools," my biggest effort to be black was to imitate the "soul strut" walk of the coolest kid in class, Eric Waddell. Eric walked with a syncopated asymmetrical stride that made it look like he was dancing to every destination. I remember when we'd all go home for lunch, I'd try to walk the same way, until my mother asked me, "Why are you walking that way?" and I was far too unconfident to lift my fist in a black power salute and say, "Cause Papa got a brand new bag!" Instead I'd offer a muffled, "I don't know, Mom" and she would say authoritatively, "No, walk your normal way. You have a fine walk that doesn't need changing!" And I would respond obediently, "Okay, Mom" and went back to my boring white kid walk. Or at least that's what I did when my mother was watching!

That same theme of going back and forth between whiteness and blackness was something all of us fifth graders knew about, and we all did it a little bit differently. Eric Waddell was "blacker" than Mark Washington in my mind, even though Mark Washington's skin was actually darker than Eric's. Eric couldn't walk any other way than his soul strut walk while Mark Washington walked like me when my mother was watching. Eric had a huge Afro and Mark had short hair. The white kids varied too. John Wolf, the only other white male kid in the class besides me, had a crew cut and I once heard him humming a pro-Vietnam War song called The Ballad of the Green Beret. This was NOT a moment of imitating his black classmates.

Although our classroom was almost entirely composed of black people, our teacher Mrs. Morris was old, white and racist, which made the blacks a de facto repressed majority, a common injustice then. Mrs. Morris insisted on a "white first" structure in her classroom, which included the requirement that the blacks behave in a subservient way to her and the four white kids, including me.

Mrs. Morris did have one redeeming quality, however; she was a chain smoker. She was so addicted to her unfiltered Chesterfield cigarettes that she had to leave the room at least once an hour and sneak down to the teacher's lounge for a smoke. "Class," she'd say, "I have to step out. You all work QUIETLY until I'm back." Sometimes it seemed she was anticipating the beauty of her huge first puff because she would add, almost kindly, as she stepped out of the room, "Thank you!"

    Mrs. Morris left us alone so often that we accepted it as normal and usually labored on whatever work sheet she'd given us. About once or twice a month, however, the Spirit would descend on Eric Waddell and the moment she'd exit, he'd jump up, strut to the door, and watch to make sure Mrs. Morris was in the teacher's lounge. The moment the coast was clear, he'd turn around and start singing and dancing and entertaining us. One of Eric's favorites was a song we all knew and loved, James Brown's mega-hit, "Say it Loud, I'm Black and I'm Proud!" The song has a call-and-response chorus, so when Eric knew we were safe, he'd look at us with his mischievous eyes and shout out like a black preacher, "Say it loud!" and we'd all shout back, "I'm black and I'm proud!!" "Say it loud," yelled Eric Waddell even louder and we'd howl "I'M BLACK AND I'M PROUD!" at the very top of our lungs! Even John Wolf joined in enthusiastically.

    Because Mrs. Morris took smoking breaks so often, we had developed an inner clock that pretty much knew how long her break would be. One time it got a little too exuberant — either that or Mrs. Morris cut her cigarette break short — because while Eric Waddell was singing and dancing and working himself into a holy lather, in she walked, about ten minutes early. She was so furious, her body was actually quivering as she commanded Eric Waddell to sit down and shut up. Not only had her classroom gotten loud while she was gone, it had gotten black! She soon took Eric out in the hallway, and when they came back in, his smile was gone. We all sat there in silence with cowered heads, breathing nervous shallow breaths. We knew Eric Waddell would very likely get paddled by the principal, but we were worried that Mrs. Morris might have us all paddled.

After several minutes of agonizing silence, Mrs. Morris finally addressed us all as if nothing had happened. "Okay class," she said, "it's time to play multiplication flashcards round robin," as if she were really excited about it and we should be too. She pulled the flash cards from the desk and the game began, as it always did at the front left of the classroom and went down each row. Mrs. Morris would turn a card around and two students could see the equation and whoever said the correct answer first went to the next desk to challenge the next student. Ronald and Calvin went first and Ronald won. At the third desk, Beverly Johnson got the answer first, as she usually did, and Ronald went back to his seat. We knew that Beverly would likely beat everyone until she got to Mark Washington, who would beat her and he would go through a row and a half of opponents until he got to me. And then I would beat him and I would go around the class and beat everyone until the game was over.

I wasn't the smartest student in the class, but I was the fastest at multiplication flashcards. That afternoon, everyone was way slower getting the correct answer because we were all so traumatized from the events of an hour earlier. Maybe it was a defense mechanism to balance my trauma, but I remember being extra confident that I would beat Mark quickly and easily and then fly around the room and be finished with round robin and Mrs. Morris's pretending that everything was fine.

All these decades later, I still remember that the flashcard Mark Washington beat me on was 5 X 6 and Mark said "thirty" almost instantaneously. There were occasions when two kids would say the answer in unison or just a fraction of a second apart, but that wasn't the case here. I was only just remembering the answer when Mark had already said it. For the first time ever, I had to sit back down in my seat and watch as Mark Washington went around the room calmly winning every card.

When Mr. Watson, the school principal, came to our class the next morning, Mrs. Morris said that although paddlings were normally given in the principal's office, our troublemakers would be paddled in front of the class so we'd see what a bad idea it was to break school rules. With great gravitas, Mrs. Morris presented to the principal Eric Waddell and Mark Washington for paddling. No one besides God could have known that Mark was going to get a paddling because he was one of the best behaved and hardest-working kids in the class. He led the class in a self-guided reading exercise called SRA, and occasionally assisted other students who needed help. When Mrs. Morris said his name, I actually wondered if I had missed a day of school recently because I couldn't think of him doing anything even slightly wrong during all the time I'd been in class with him.

It was only the moment before his actual paddling that I figured out that Mark was being punished for beating me at round robin the day before. Mrs. Morris said, "Mr. Watson, Mark Washington has been disruptive and disrespectful to his classmates" and right as she said "classmates," she looked straight at me with a conspiratorial "we-whites-have-to-stick-together" nod. I just froze. I'm sure Mrs. Morris was as baffled by the horror on my face as I was by her ability to humiliate one of her best students for working extra hard at math.

Eric Waddell and Mark Washington got five hard licks each. Eric was first and walked back to his chair like nothing had happened and certainly nothing had disturbed or altered his cool strut walk. I felt a tiny bit of relief, at least until Mark got paddled. I could see the pain register on his whole body and when he walked back to his seat I saw tears on his cheeks. I felt my face quiver like I was going to cry too so I opened my eyes as wide as they would go and filled my lungs as full as they would go to make tears impossible. Tears may not have flowed, but I cried on the inside.

Something broke in me that day and I learned the destructive power of an emotion that I hadn't really felt before: guilt. Because in addition to the confusion, fear, frustration and anger, I kept thinking that if I had said "thirty" before Mark, he wouldn't have gotten paddled. If I were black, like 24 out of 28 kids in class were, he wouldn't have been paddled. I even accused myself of not having done more to protect Eric Waddell. My desk was closer to the classroom door. Why hadn't I kept watch yesterday while we sang "I'm Black and I'm Proud" so we all would have been safe? I could have prevented two paddlings with one single act.

Of the first eighteen years of my life, I still remember that day as the day when I was no longer a child. Not to say I was an adult, or even an adolescent, but the kid in me was dead. To compound matters, I made that child's death my own fault and then carried the guilt and blame for years.

My parents took me out of Cornell Heights and put me in a private school less than a month later, right in the middle of the school year. This was long enough ago that no one would have said that a ten-year-old was suffering from depression and PTSD, but my grades were plummeting and my mother and Mrs. Morris had been warring over how the class was being taught and disciplined.

It was good to change schools, but in some ways the damage was done. Although I would go on to get a BA and a master's degree, I never enjoyed being in school again. It was like going to the dentist — something I had to do, but didn't enjoy. I crammed enough credits into three years of high school so that I could graduate a year early, and then, rather than rush off to college, I spent a year working a number of jobs and healing some of the long-term effects of 11 years of schooling.

Without a doubt, the most healing minutes of that year were the few I spent talking with Eric Waddell, whom I saw as I was weeding a garden in Dayton View, where we both still lived. I spotted him walking up Otterbein Avenue, and even after seven years of not seeing him I saw that his soul strut had not only been retained, but improved. Walking gave Eric Waddell joy and his balletic motion seemed to be an invitation for everyone else to celebrate as well. From a ways off, I shouted, "I'd recognize that cool Eric Waddell walk even if it were thirty years from now!" and I went to greet him with the same 1970 dap handshake we did in fifth grade.

Without spending a second on niceties, I cut

straight to the chase. "Eric," I said, "I want to apologize for not defending you in fifth grade. If I hadn't been so scared and shocked, I would have insisted on getting paddled that same day you did, but I didn't even think of that possibility until about five years later! But for whatever it's worth, thinking of you and the paddling day still makes me angry and I feel terrible and guilty I was such a chicken! I can't even imagine how pissed off you must be! And Mark Washington, don't even get me started on that shit..." Eric Waddell jumped in here, "Whoa! Chris-man, stop! I'm not pissed off about any of all that and you don't owe anybody an apology!" Eric just started shaking his head and his hands and it was like his whole body was warming up to saying something really important. "First," he said, "all that was a long, long time ago but check it out!" Eric held up his arms like a preacher making an important point, "Look here," and he paused and spread his arms first to the sky and then to the whole neighborhood. "How could I stay angry about something like that when GOD MADE SO MUCH GOOD?" He gave me a second to reflect and then put the cherry on top, "And Mark Washington is going to Ohio University this fall on a full academic scholarship so you know God gave him the victory over Mrs. Morris!"

    Those mischievous eyes glowed with joy watching me hear the news. "And that's the same Mrs. Morris who died about two, maybe three months back, may she rest in peace." For a millisecond, I thought he was making this up, but I could see that it was as true as a sunset. In the next millisecond, I bet Eric saw something like relief and joy on my face — like hearing the wicked witch had melted — but to steer me away from that vengefulness,

Eric Waddell doubled down on pure Grace by saying, "Chris, my brother, it's so much easier to forgive when you remember everyone is doing their best, even Marilyn Morris."

Oh my God, not only had Eric Waddell remembered Mrs. Morris's first name, but he had just spoken it calmly and lovingly! I was stunned by his capacity for forgiveness and his complete lack of anger and resentment. Eric had been a true victim of injustice and here he was ministering to me and encouraging me to not let my unforgiven-ness block the possibility of true joy.

After a great sermon like that, spending time on chit-chat would have been anti-climactic I guess, because Eric continued on his way soon after. I could hear him as he started humming as he danced up the street. Maybe he felt me watching, because he suddenly and smoothly did a half spin and faced me while soul-strutting backwards. Eric Waddell pointed at me and yelled "Say it loud!" and with childlike joy and adult vocal power, I raised my right hand in a fist and roared, "I'M BLACK AND I'M PROUD!!" even though we both knew I'd never been either.

Nuclear Obsession

It was in the fall of 1982 when I had the great and terrible luck of registering for a one credit mini-course called Nuclear Arms Proliferation. Ronald Reagan was the president and in the year plus that he'd been in office, nuclear spending had soared and the policy of "mutually assured destruction," or MAD, had gotten even crazier or "MADDER." Truth is, I really wouldn't have known very much, or worried about, nuclear weapons if it had not been for this one course. And, ironically, a big motive for my taking the course was that I assumed that it would be an extremely easy credit! But although the reading load was light and the assignments sparse, this one little itty-bitty mini-course would require more effort and have more effect on my life than any other course I took to get my bachelor's degree.

Predictably, the material was presented in a way that reflected liberal arts values at a liberal institution, the University of Michigan. We were presented with facts and figures and the full history of the nuclear arms race, as well as its escalation, but the professor added a tragic, "isn't this ignorant beyond all imagination" subjectivity to all the material. He not only taught us about how many warheads could be delivered on each ICBM (intercontinental ballistic missile), but also made no effort to hide his rage as he shared the news of a nun in the Detroit area who had been jailed after protesting outside of a cruise missile jet propeller factory. The right-wing judge in the case ensured that her sentencing would extend over the Christmas holiday so she would miss celebrating Christmas with her sisters at the Convent. This was proof in the professor's mind that before the world ended in nuclear holocaust, all human decency would perish first. I confess I was positive he was right, and became hopeless and depressed.

The course only met for ninety minutes per week and had an easy syllabus, but even with this moderate workload, the amount of mental energy the course consumed became oppressive for me. Within a month, I found myself thinking of nuclear arms pretty much every waking hour of the day. It prevented my falling asleep quickly at night and when I'd finally get to sleep I would frequently dream about nuclear bombs falling, sometimes right over nearby Detroit, forty miles east of Ann Arbor and the university.

The obsession was also something I was unable to keep to myself. At first I shared the weapons race information with my friends in a sane and reasonable manner and with a reasonable tone, but as my obsession increased, I would speak of little else and my tone became more strident. I could turn every situation and conversation around to the topic of nuclear arms. In a bar, I'd lament, "Here we are drinking a pitcher of beer when we should be out protesting 24/7!" And in academic classes, I'd derail good discussions with comments like, "Isn't it a bit naïve to sit here luxuriating in Shakespeare sonnets when it's likely we'll all die of a nuclear blast or from radiation fallout soon after?"

As I spread gloom, some of my friends would ignore me, others would try to coax me away from the topic with humor, and perhaps the wisest of all avoided me completely during my most obsessive phase. A tiny part of me knew I was going crazy, but the bigger part of me denied it. I knew that it was actually funny when my friend said, "We'll go end the arms race after one more pitcher, Chris" and everybody laughed, except me. There was still a little part of me that wanted to laugh with them, but was unable.

Very worst of all, I started becoming a hater. I hated Ronald Reagan, I hated the Pentagon, I hated every defense contractor, I hated anybody who had voted for any Republican, and anybody who had profited even slightly from American corporations that had even the slightest connection to the Department of Defense. At one point I even caught myself thinking negative and judgmental thoughts about Albert Einstein (as in, "How could he be so foolish as to share his insights with such a flawed species as humankind?!").

I certainly wasn't aware at the time that my level of self-righteousness and judgment of others were an extreme form of self-hatred. I actually thought I was okay and others were the problem. I wasn't okay, however. When my obsession could get no larger and there were no more additional moments in the day to feel frightened and when I was barely able to concentrate on the academic requirements of my other three courses — all four credit courses — an unusual event happened.

In the middle of the night, I sat up to discover that my stomach was on fire. Not actual fire that could consume my t-shirt but a fire that somehow was more real than earthly fire — like a super-reality. And because I wasn't feeling burned and my clothes weren't on fire, I was able to give it my full attention without fear. When I shared the story later, people asked if I was awake, or asleep and dreaming. And the answer is, strangely, both and neither. The experience was more real than the most realistic event awake or the most vivid dream or vision when sleeping.

People often talk about the voice of God, but there are times when God communicates in a modality that transcends voices and words. This was one of those nights. As I watched the fire on my stomach burn, I knew wisdom and instruction were being imparted to me somehow. There was no sense of time so I have no sense of whether I acquired the wisdom instantaneously or whether it took an hour. I do know that when I woke up the next morning from a miraculously deep and amazing sleep, I felt a peace and calm that I had never known. I was also positive that I had received information and instruction in the course of the night, instruction that if put it into words would be as if God had said something like this: "In your lifetime there will be no nuclear exchange, nor will there be any nuclear holocaust and to worry about either is a complete waste of time! I appreciate your passion, but it needs to be entirely redirected elsewhere." And then it was as if God had added affectionately, "PLEASE GET A LIFE!"

As if this weren't enough in terms of providing total peace of mind, the very next night I had yet another dream. It was short and far more realistic and memorable than a normal dream — like it was perfectly recorded and in high-def. In the dream an old man in his late 70s or 80s was lying in a hospital bed. I heard him make a long — and final — exhalation and as he did, I could see a living shape of him, a human shape made of pure light, sit up from the body in the bed and lift upwards. It was then that the dream was like a camera zooming in to close-up and I could see that the corpse was me! With complete calm and with a feeling that was almost joyful, I realized I was witnessing my own death 50 or 60 years in advance. It was really clear that I had not been killed by a nuclear bomb in the 1980s because for me to have been as old as I was in the dream, humankind would have to have made it at least to the year 2040!

From that day forward and throughout all the intervening years, I never feared nuclear arms again. I truly believe that God wanted me to live and grow without being haunted by them. It's not that I don't think these weapons are dangerous or that there is not a need for diplomacy. I do, but I realize that calmer and wiser minds will prevail and that there will be no nuclear exchange. It was not my life purpose to battle President Reagan in the 1980s nor any politician since. As God requested, I did "get a life" and I've tried to live it as beautifully as the Shakespeare sonnets I studied with renewed vigor back in the late fall of 1982.

Postscript:

Sonnet 15

When I consider everything that grows
Holds in perfection but a little moment,
That this huge stage presenteth nought but shows
Whereon the stars in secret influence comment;
When I perceive that men as plants increase,
Cheered and cheque'd even by the self-same sky,
Vaunt in their youthful sap, at height decrease,
And wear their brave state out of memory;
Then the conceit of this inconstant stay
Sets you most rich in youth before my sight,
Where wasteful Time debateth with Decay,
To changes your day of yourh to sullied night;
And all in war with Time for love of you,
As he takes from you, I engraft you new.

- William Shakespeare

Adrenal Gland

    In the early 1990s, people would come over to my house in Key West to experience a process that I have never named. Other people gave names to what I did, however: Some called it Reiki, others called it "energy work," others called it Chi Gong therapy and Christians would sometimes call it the gift of healing from the Holy Spirit. I even researched some of these traditions after I heard about them (and studied Chi Gong in Miami and in Hong Kong many years later), but with my closest friends and my wife Bettina, I would still refer to these sessions simply as "back things," because one of the few constants of the process was that I would begin by putting my hands on, or near, people's backs above their shoulder blades.

    The results varied, as did the actual process. Invariably, themes or ideas would come to me intuitively. Sometimes I shared these insights aloud and there was a lot of verbal communication — sometimes one-sided and sometimes dialogical. Other times the sessions were entirely silent and I would concentrate on the flow of energy that I could sense with my hands. This energy could also be increased, decreased, transformed or relocated, with the goal always being an increase of wellness — body, mind and soul — of the participant.

Because we also practiced deep, focused breathing in "back things," a high percentage of participants would report that they felt greater calm, a reduction of tension or anxiety, and an increase of joy during and after the session — very similar to the benefits of meditation. Also common were reports of just feeling lighter or less stressed, and in some cases, people claimed physical healing or spiritual deliverance, either instantaneously or soon after the session.

Because Bettina and I ran a successful business, doing the healing work was actually a pleasant break from the routine and the monotony of our hand-painted clothing company. Painting and selling clothing was a "living," and doing sessions was a "calling."

Occasionally, someone would ask if I charged anything for the sessions and I would let them know that I had decided not to accept money for a number of reasons. First, it was a tradition and I would have felt strange charging someone knowing that their friend had received the same service for free. Second, Bettina and I were already making more money than we were spending. And last, while flipping through an old Bible, I had bumped in to a passage in which Jesus had said to his disciples, "Heal the sick, cleanse the lepers, raise the dead, cast out devils: freely ye have received, freely give." Pretty much any one of these reasons would have been enough for me never to charge money, but the three together made my resolve an iron-clad rule.

Or at least iron-clad until Katherine came along. Katherine was a friend of an acquaintance and someone I had never met before the day she called to request a meeting with me. With confidence and clarity, she said she had heard about my work and was absolutely positive that I would be able to heal her of a very rare condition, which, if it continued unchanged, would require surgery to remove one of her adrenal glands. Before I even had a chance to offer my normal corrective — that I don't heal anybody, only God and the person's faith do that — she was telling me how great I was and how anxious she was for me to do my "miraculous healing work" with her. To top it all off, this flattery was being delivered by a contralto voice with the slightest French accent — imagine if Lauren Bacall had grown up in Paris with North American parents. When Katherine asked how soon she could come over, I said, "Now would be perfect!"

It actually took Katherine an hour to arrive although it was only a ten-minute drive from the high-end luxury neighborhood of Key West where she was snowbirding (living in the north in the summer and in Florida for the winter) to the working class part of town where I lived year-round. I heard her car as she pulled up in the gravel parking area in front of our half of the duplex and looked out to see her exiting her new white BMW. Tall, thin, well-dressed, and with the perfect amount of sexy going on, Katherine was what I imagine most women hope they look like at forty. And it was Katherine's interest in preserving her great looks that was the primary reason we were meeting. The biggest concern she had about her scheduled surgery was the fact that it would require a 10-12 inch incision from her belly button around to her back — an incision she dramatically referred to as a "watermelon cut." She had no doubts at all about the surgery being successful if she had it, but she wanted to be healed without any cutting. She didn't want to endure a long healing time, but above all else, she didn't want the permanent scar on her lower abdomen. I actually was fairly sympathetic but I do remember that I quietly hoped that when I was as old as Katherine (I was 33), I wouldn't be so looks conscious.

After refusing my offer of fresh-squeezed grapefruit juice, Katherine parked herself on the couch. She folded her long legs, crossing them at the ankles, and resumed her pitch. I learned that her surgery was scheduled in Montreal, and that she would be returning there in early May. She saved a special topic for last; although she knew I didn't typically charge for my sessions, she would "insist" on paying me for my time and skill. "That won't be necessary," I said, "and I kind of have a rule against it."

A debate began that I would go on to lose. First, she had somehow learned that I regularly traded my sessions with a licensed massage therapist who took my family out for sails on his boat. Since there was no money involved, and because neither he nor I kept track of the sessions, I told Katherine that I felt like that didn't count as "payment." "Okay," she said, "let's not call it a payment, but rather a gift! You can take my money and hire any licensed massage therapist you want, including your friend, and all will be well." Perhaps the most persuasive of all her arguments, however, was her claim that she "would be more open to my healing powers" if she paid me and that my work would be "far more effective." She really seemed to believe it.

And she was so clear about all her beliefs and opinions. I think my subconscious knew I was out-matched but rather than confess my confusion or ask Katherine to give me a moment to sort out my thoughts, I just started agreeing to everything she asked. My ego took over too and I wondered to myself, "Maybe she's right — maybe I do have some 'miraculous powers!' What if I actually am as rare and special as Katherine seems to think?" And to my personal vanity, I added a pinch of self-justifying greed. "If this woman wants to buy me and my family a week's worth of groceries for a half hour of my time," I thought, "why would I waste another half hour debating her?" Maybe if I were more like her, I considered, I'd also be driving a BMW 525i like hers and not an Oldsmobile station wagon! I accepted her check — she wanted to pay in advance — and we scheduled a session for the next afternoon at her home.

From my perspective, the session was the worst I'd ever done, although Katherine clearly loved it. The unhealthy energies resisted the usual readjustments that I'd come to think of as automatic. Because they were "stubborn," I found myself unable to sweep or brush them away from her and instead I did something that I rarely did, and always cautiously. On rare occasions, I'd used my forearms like they were spiritual vacuum cleaners to suck the bad energy out of the person and then go outside and shake the energies away, just like emptying the dirt canister on our Hoover upright. I did that during Katherine's session, but on each occasion when I stepped outside to empty myself, I felt like my arms would only half empty, leaving lots of un-wellness in me as I went back to work on her.

At about thirty minutes into the session, I sensed that we were finished, although at this point I would have written someone else a check just to take away the agitation in my body, mind and soul that I had just absorbed and was unable to shake off. Katherine was glowingly happy and incredibly grateful and wanted to share her understanding of the experience. "Amazing!" she said. "Several times I pictured you as a powerful spiritual vacuum cleaner, just sucking all the illness out of me and leaving me spotless!"

Had I been wiser, I would have asked myself that day why I had been so self-sacrificing to a complete stranger, but instead I remember thinking, "If she's happy, I'm happy." And had I been more self-aware, I probably would have started a fast and begun a prayer vigil until I felt completely cleansed of whatever I'd just vacuumed up. Instead, I just basked for a few more minutes in Katherine's praise and said goodbye. As I got in my car, I felt a sudden need to go to the closest ocean water I could find and jump in. Strangely, the closest ocean water (with public access, anyway) was mangy Dog Beach, a twenty-foot spit of sand in between an upscale restaurant and a four-star hotel. I parked, hid my keys on the Oldsmobile's back tire, and rushed to the water, jumping in with all my clothes on — just me, a hippie and his two smiling dogs!

I felt better after the swim. My arms hurt in a weird way that I'd never felt before, but I assumed whatever it was would fix itself. I thought of Katherine briefly when I deposited her check, but didn't revisit the event otherwise. When Katherine called a few months later to let me know that the hormonal imbalance had been completely corrected and her surgery canceled, it as if I were re-watching a movie of the conversation. More than a déjà vu feeling, it was like discussing events that had taken place decades before. I remember saying how happy I was for her and enjoyed hearing once more, with my usual blend of insecurity and egotism, about how gifted and great I was!

I could have received Katherine's compliments in a more constructive manner, but I went on to discover that one of the reasons Katherine and I ever crossed paths was because she was going to teach me how to be that person who never confused the gift with the Giver. Had I known then how truly blessed I was, I am sure that I never would have experienced all the health challenges of the next seven years. But the God of Grace wanted me to learn that a posture of gratitude was better than aggrandizement.

Medical histories are rarely interesting, so I'll speed through the next seven years. The ache in my arm slowly moved to my chest. I took aspirin, which did nothing. I was diagnosed with high blood pressure. I took high blood pressure medication, which did nothing. An almost total lack of potassium in my system was said to be the cause of the high blood pressure. I took potassium pills, about 25 times the daily recommended requirement, but my body didn't retain it. I was tested for diabetes (negative) and told to not eat salt. I stopped drinking my daily café con leches and all other forms of caffeine, but I didn't improve at all.

In the sixth year of being sick, my wife and I decided to move from Key West to Sewanee, Tennessee, for me to attend seminary, so I clearly was still thinking long term. And as I have discovered a number of times in my life, so was God. Within a few months of our move, I was hospitalized with chest pains so severe I could hardly breathe. One of the nurses at the hospital read me the riot act on my health, and with Bettina listening, told us that our single highest priority needed to be the diagnosis and treatment of my problem because I could easily die at any moment of cardiac arrest. (I still remember her saying that she'd "seen higher potassium levels in anorexic corpses" and how impressed I was by her dramatics!)

In forty-eight hours, my wife had researched every cardiologist in Chattanooga and Nashville and began calling their offices. Because it was a weekend, she left message after message on machines with our contact information. At about nine o'clock on a Sunday night, she phoned a Nashville doctor, ready to leave the same life-or-death message when, miraculously, a live voice answered with, "This is Joe Fredi." Dr. Fredi and my wife talked for nearly forty-five minutes, and when Bettina hung up, she had a "just spoke with an angel" glow about her that brought peace and reassurance to our entire household.

That same week, I checked into the best hospital in Tennessee, the Vanderbilt University Medical Center in Nashville. I had a battery of tests, and finally received a diagnosis from Dr. Fredi. I had hyperaldosteronism, a rare (one or two people in a million) hormonal imbalance caused by a hyper-producing adrenal gland that would need to be removed as soon as possible. As most people who know me will confirm, I've always had a dense streak, and I will literally not see the most obvious fact in the world. As proof of that, I never once thought of Katherine nor was reminded of her healing session seven years earlier until the moment I was told I would have my "right adrenal gland surgically removed." And only then, at that very second, did I remember Katherine's phrase, "watermelon cut."

And then one by one, I remembered details about Katherine that seemed to be more than coincidental. She was 40 then and I was 40 now. She had mentioned it was an extremely rare hormonal occurrence, and that "less than two in a million" actually had to have surgery to correct it. When Bettina and I spoke later, she reminded me of an occurrence I had completely forgotten. I had once half-jokingly said that I was going to "suck a chest cold right out of Maya" (our daughter, who at the time was about 18 months old) and with my mouth about an inch above her shoulder blades, I inhaled deeply until my intuition said "all clear." Within an hour, Maya was fever-less and playing, and I was sniffling and using the VapoRub we'd just bought for her.

I also remembered how Katherine had been one of the last sessions in which I ever intentionally allowed what I felt was harmful energy to enter me past my wrists. It would be almost impossible for the energy not to linger a bit on or around my fingers, but Katherine was the last time I acted as a human vacuum cleaner.

I'll just cut to the chase here. I came to believe that I somehow had absorbed the root causes as well as all the symptoms of Katherine's disease, and when I did so, she no longer had either. I had my right adrenal gland removed three weeks later and I too healed, and quickly. And just like Katherine had achieved seven years earlier, I had normal blood pressure, normal potassium levels (without any medications or supplements) and my energy level increased.

 Although there have been times over the years when I have asked myself how I could have been so dumb in so many ways and needlessly lost an adrenal gland and damaged my heart, I am grateful now for every facet of that experience. I count my lost adrenal gland as the "tuition" I had to pay to learn countless valuable lessons about how to live better and to be a better steward of God's gifts. I always say that one can discern God's will when every party benefits, when it is win-win for everyone. I truly believe that was the case with Katherine and me. We both got sick and got healed in a way that felt miraculous to us both.

 Time provided a bit of serendipity to this story as well. In the seven years that had passed between Katherine's surgery being canceled and my surgery being performed, laparoscopic procedures, including internal video cameras, had gone from experimental to commonplace. So although I did have my adrenal gland removed, it was through four pencil-width holes, none more than 3/8 of an inch across. Katherine and I were both healed and we both avoided the dreaded watermelon cut! And like Katherine, I was still concerned enough about my looks that I was very happy not to have the scar.

 As if there weren't enough karmic energy and connection between Katherine and me, I would come to learn even more from the 90 total minutes we interacted in life. I believe the most valuable thing I provided to her was that I pointed her to the Source of what she perceived were my innate abilities. I invited her to understand that if God were the well and she were the garden, I was, at best, a decent watering can.

And for all the miracles that Katherine authored in my life, her biggest gift to me was something that she modeled so well and that I am still working on 25 years later, and it is this: Katherine was a confident, bright and beautiful woman but far rarer about her was her extraordinary clarity about what she wanted and needed in life and her ability to make it happen. In the school of life, she got A+ in these subjects and helped me realize that I'd been getting mostly C's and D's! However remedial a student I was to start, I have been studying and emulating Katherine's strengths ever since.

    Oh, and I still do "sessions," which I still have no name for. Fortunately, in the last 25 years, no one has compared the feeling of my work to a vacuum cleaner and I believe that doing the work has never had anything but desirable effects on me. And since Katherine, I've never once accepted payment. What I was given freely, I'm still sharing for free.

Born to Fly: Bruce Springsteen and the AMC Pacer

There were a lot of reasons that my sister and I were airborne in an AMC Pacer doing 100 miles per hour on — or several feet above, actually — a country road that night. I mean reasons beyond the obvious physics of the situation since every car ever made would have been airborne had they crested the same hill at the same speed at that same place in southwestern Ohio. Not only were we in a hurry, but we were happy about why we were in one! We had decided, spur of the moment, to attend a Bruce Springsteen concert that evening in Oxford, Ohio, and knew that the faster we went, the better our tickets would be.

That there were even tickets available came as a surprise. It was October, 1976, and Bruce had recently grown from a local club-playing New Jersey hero to a burgeoning world phenomenon. I'd been out of town when tickets (which were still pre-printed on paper and couldn't be bought online since there was no internet yet) had gone on sale weeks before, and when I thought about attending later, I assumed they were long sold out.

So while listening to WTUE, the top-40 hits station of Dayton, I was stunned when Lawanna Johnny said, "Here's a little something for all of you heading out to hear The Boss tonight at Millett Hall, and the good people there wanted me to tell you that there are still lots of great seats available! Oh yeah," the deep-voiced disc jockey continued, "we're gonna take the Thuunnnnder Road down to hear Bruce tonight in Oxford, baby!" and when Lawanna said "thunder" it sounded like thunder!

I instantly decided to attend and the second I did, it was like a speed-optimizing force guided my every action. Rather than wash the paint brushes and roller I was using (I was the hired help at a remodeling job up the street from where I lived), I just pulled the plastic drop-cloth over everything and pushed all the air out. Rather than washing my hands, I saved another minute by grabbing a bunch of paper towels to keep my fingers from touching the car's steering wheel and stick-shift knob.

When I got home, I shouted to my sister Constance, "I'm going to hear Springsteen and leaving this second, wanna come?" And in less than three minutes we were on our way. Neither of us was dressed up. I hadn't even changed my painters' pants when I grabbed a warmer shirt.

That was the beauty of Springsteen, whose music said "come as you are" because that's what rock 'n roll requires. Bruce was like an antidote to the encroaching disco dress-up craze that was just arriving in Ohio. The most dressed-up thing about us that night was our car choice — my dad's brand new AMC Pacer, which my sister and I could use as long as we left the keys to either my Triumph or her MG.

Although both of our bright red sports cars screamed British cool, we wanted the Pacer because neither of our cars was as reliable nor, more important, as fast as the Pacer. (And yes, I did know the actual top speed on all three of them — it's a Midwestern guy thing.) So to get to Springsteen as quickly as possible, the right choice was the shiny monkey-shit brown 1976 Pacer that still had the new-car smell — the same new-car fragrance that I was ruining with the Marlboros I chain-smoked (another Midwestern guy thing, at least back then).

I pretty much knew the way to where we were going and also knew that there were little towns on US Route 35 that balanced their budgets on out-of-town speeders — guys just like me, if I let them. So, because I knew we would need to travel southwest, I chose unpatrolled farm roads, paved but only about a lane and a half wide, to go west and then south and then west and then south again in the familiar grid pattern that characterizes almost the entire rural Midwest. It was too late in the evening for farm traffic and we'd have the roads to ourselves, so I figured I'd go as fast as the car would go and all would be well.

And life was just about as good as it could get. WTUE was playing more Springsteen, Born to Run was blasting, and we were singing along "the amusement park rises cold and stark, kids are huddled in the beach in the mist. I wanna die with you Wendy in the streets tonight in an ever-lasting kiss!" God, could this man ever write songs!

Had I been paying more attention to driving and not singing, I would have slowed down a bit when I first spotted the hill ahead, but my attention was on repeating the words "Tramps like us, baby we were bor-orn to runnnn!" and taking a huge puff off my cigarette when the famous Born to Run guitar lick gave us a break from singing. Ahhh, exhaling a big lungful of smoke and driving a car doing 100 MPH with one hand — I doubt incautiousness and overconfidence were ever as perfectly united as they were in the 17-year-old me. When we crested that hill and the Pacer became airborne, something worse than an oncoming car was in front of us; our headlights shone on a field of dry cornstalks. As the hood of the car lowered and the road ahead was again visible, we realized we were less than 150 feet from a stop sign and a dead-end "T" in the road. (Signage is nearly non-existent on farm roads, so there had been no "STOP AHEAD" sign.) At the speed the car was traveling, I would have needed ten times the distance I had to stop the car and even with a drag-car racer's parachute, I wouldn't have been able to slow the car enough to make the left turn safely. Going straight into the corn field would have been fine IF there hadn't been a deep ditch between the road and the field.

    And in a millisecond, these things happened: 1) I heard my sister gasp, the inhaled kind so sharp and sudden it makes a loud sound. 2) I actually located the spot on the embankment where we would make impact and our car would be reduced to an accordion and 3) I made a mental note to myself that brake pedals don't do anything when a car is in the air.

    And instantaneously, like someone had cut ten feet of film from a movie, we were at the edge of a road, on a grassy shoulder coming to a stop from a very slow speed. My foot was still on the brakes, but they were working fine now and we came to a stop, utterly safe. Somehow we had been "relocated" to the place where we would have been had I made the left turn at that T intersection and driven a mile down the road closer to Oxford. And this relocation consumed no time. My fingers were just as clenched on the wheel as when we had been airborne and the cigarette in the car's ashtray was still lit with about two-thirds left to smoke.

Less than a second before, I was in the air, foreseeing my sister's and my death — a death that would have been a result of wanting to get a slightly better seat at a rock concert! — and now, we weren't dead, we weren't injured and my dad's car was still perfect and new. On one level I think I knew that if I learned the explanation of this miraculous relocating force, my brain would have exploded, so I shut the thought down and acted as if nothing unusual had happened. I casually reached for my cigarette but before I could shift the Pacer into first gear and resume our trip, my sister said, "What just happened?" I could feel her looking at me but I was unable to return her look. I knew that I wouldn't be able to deal with the look of wonder or confusion or curiosity about what had just happened and what had miraculously NOT HAPPENED — that we had been saved from a sure and certain death, which would have been my fault. I didn't know the answer to her question and was pretty sure I didn't want to know, so I quickly and faux-casually said "got me," kept looking straight ahead and promptly forgot the whole thing. And it stayed forgotten, at least by me, for decades.

++++++++++++++++++

Bruce Springsteen truly was "The Boss" that evening and the E Street Band was everything we hoped they might be and more. We got good seats and were in them five minutes before the band opened the set with Springsteen's biggest hit, Born to Run. We knew right then that we were seeing something new because EVERY rock band in history saved their biggest hit for late in the set, or even last, but Springsteen was confident or crazy enough to open with his current radio hit. So there we were, singing Born to Run, again, but this time with 3,200 other people in a theatre that wasn't even entirely full.

Thirty-five years later, my sister would tell me that even during the show, she wondered back to the absolutely impossible thing that had happened on the way there but I had already put it out of my mind completely. I'd learned to repress things so totally that they never crossed my mind again unless God insisted they did. In the same way that I managed to make it to forty years old before I remembered the sexual abuse of my childhood, I made it into my early fifties before my sister asked me at the end of a long phone call if I remembered that night in 1976 when we went to see Springsteen, and, for the first time since that night, I let myself remember every detail.

And the details of her remembrance of the story were identical to mine. Ask any police officer gathering evidence only moments after an occurrence, and they will tell you that people will report wildly different accounts of the same event; but my memory of the miraculous and life-saving relocation of the car that night was identical to my sister's. Constance also reminded me of other things about the night that she had regularly cherished in her memory but I had not. When she mentioned the working-guys at the concert who had seats directly in front of us, I did remember them too. She said she could still picture one of them wearing a Sohio (Standard Oil of Ohio — a common gas and service station brand in the 1970s) work shirt and how he and his friend exchanged a "yeah bro" look exactly when Springsteen belted out, "I wanna know if love is wild girl, I wanna know if love is real!"

Constance also remembered another story I'd entirely forgotten. About a year after the Springsteen show, after I'd moved to Michigan to start college, I had talked her into coming with me to try to get a job at the local paper, The Ann Arbor News. On a chilly Sunday night, we left our parents' house in Dayton and began the four-hour trip in my 1974 Triumph Spitfire. As we left town, we got to a spot where the houses ended and the farm fields began and I reached to switch on the radio. I pushed the mechanical pre-set button for WTUE, and the second the radio came on, we heard the opening piano chords and harmonica to Thunder Road. And on that night, I was able to look my sister right in the eye and accept the idea that it was a "sign" even if I didn't let myself remember the greater miracle of the year before. Life was good, we were singing along and happily riding — at the speed limit — into endless Grace and Blessing, Thunder and Mercy.

Kim and the Ouija Board

I'd always been skeptical of Ouija boards until that night in Brooklyn, NY. Although my sisters and I had a board when we were children, I don't remember receiving any valuable messages from it. And after playing with it once or twice, we retired our Ouija board. It stayed neatly folded in its box, which slowly flattened at the bottom of the stack of other board games we played more regularly, like Risk, Clue and Monopoly.

But when I saw the board at my friends' apartment twenty years later, I was intrigued. It had caught my attention a number of times before simply because it was so lovingly constructed. Rather than purchase the official Hasbro cardboard game, my friend Dave had constructed his own board from an 18" square piece of solid wood. And for an indicator, he used a clear 4 oz. juice glass. I remember thinking that it would take more effort (either from us or from the spirits) to push the glass around this wooden board than the slippery indicator that came with the Hasbro board edition. Oh well, I reassured myself, even if it moves slowly or just sits there,

there's plenty of beer!

    Dave, his roommate Nick, and I positioned ourselves around the board, put our fingers on the glass and asked, "Is anyone there?" and the indicator went straight to YES. Then, without asking it another question, it started darting around the board, stopping at letters and numbers that pretty much meant nothing to anyone. Dave, our Ouija expert, acted as secretary, recording every letter on a fresh legal pad. When it stopped, Dave said, "We didn't understand you. Can we start with something simpler, like what is your name?" And bang, the glass raced from K to I to M! We double-checked with her and said, "So you're Kim, right?" and the juice glass flew to "YES."

    And from that second on, I believed that the spirit of Kim was there with us and that she could communicate with us. The main reason I believed so suddenly was because of the feeling I had of another person being in the room with us — it's as if we all had shifted to accommodate Kim's presence. That and the fact that there was no way in the world the letters K-I-M would have spelled themselves out that quickly unless the boys and I had all decided in advance to spell Kim and had practiced it a few times.

    Before we asked Kim any questions about ourselves or the next realm, we asked her to tell us more about herself. In a format much like the children's game 20 Questions, we figured out that Kim had been from Detroit, had died young and was not angry or unhappy about where she was now. What Dave already seemed to know, but I needed to learn, was that actual dates and ages are not allowed to be communicated. Although it seemed as if Kim were trying to tell us her age when she died, it was never clear whether the first number in her age was a 2 or a 3. The glass would stop in between the two numbers, or in the general area, but never lined up precisely.

This same thing happened when I asked Kim how old I would live to be. The glass kept wobbling between the 7 and 8, even going to the top of the board, which we perceived as "neutral space" in between each try. "Kim," I asked finally, "is it accurate to say that I am going to die at 77, 78, 87 or 88?" Kim said YES immediately. Nick jumped in, "Uh, Kim, just to be clear, the rest of us don't want to know when we're dying!" and Dave nodded in agreement. "Of that day and hour, no one knows," Dave said, and I remember thinking how poetic Dave was since I had no idea he was quoting the Bible.

We would get the best answers when we didn't ask for precise facts. Rather than ask her exact age or date of death, we asked, "You were young when you died, right?" and Kim gave a definitive and instantaneous "YES." We discussed these "blocked" messages regarding death dates among ourselves and thought that maybe there is some heavenly law that prohibits that information from being communicated. We thought that it might be a way of preventing damage from knowing things we shouldn't; after all, we could contact Kim's relatives and maybe freak them out, even if our intentions were kind. Dave mentioned that there were biblical warnings against using this information to manipulate others or to create dependency, so these filters actually felt holy and sacred rather than frustrating or limiting. It felt as if we were always learning the "right" amount; the filters allowed the perfect amount and quality of information to come through. For example, we could not get a clear spelling on Kim's last name although we could ascertain it might be Polish since S-K-I came at the end. "Kim," we finally asked, "we're not getting your name, but is it something Polish?" YES said Kim immediately.

    I know this may sound creepy, but not half an hour into our "conversation," I had a huge crush on Kim. She seemed so earnest and good and confident but still a tiny bit shy. I had started by dominating the conversation, but instead of wanting information about myself or the wide world, I just kept wanting to know more about Kim. With yes and no questions, we learned that Kim had grown up in Dearborn and that her parents and siblings were all still alive. She told us she used to have light brown hair, blue eyes and was medium height. (Yes, I did actually ask a dead person who no longer had a body what she looked like! Yes, I was that superficial!).

    "Kim," I said, "I'm not going to even ask you if you were totally sexy, because I already know you were!" to which Kim gave her fastest and clearest response. The glass raced to NO and then, just as quickly, the glass spelled out N-O-T. I felt stupid, and a bit chastised, but still said for Kim, my friends and all the world to hear, "I know that's the wrongest thing you are going to say all night — 'cause you are totally sexy! You are nothing but hot, lady!"

    And I meant it. I wanted to go to where Kim was and kiss the lips and hug the body she no longer had. Back then, I thought that love could only be demonstrated through flirting, conquest and then some kind of passionate consummation. Kim and my guy friends knew better. Not only did Kim discourage my flirting, so did Dave and Nick. The good news, at least, is that everyone was nice about it. A little embarrassed, and more confused, I walked to the fridge to grab another Beck's and decided to just listen for a while. And with the tiny amount of self-reflection I possessed, I did ask myself, "What is it that you are desiring so much from a ghost?"

As for my friends, their conversation with Kim was mostly about how to optimize their activities in life. We were all aspiring artists, so Nick the bass player asked Kim if he should continue to play in two bands or concentrate on just his favorite and spend the extra hours playing the upright (acoustic bass). Dave, an aspiring screenwriter, asked craft-related questions, too. Nick and I also learned from Dave that Kim could hear your silent thoughts as easily as when you spoke them aloud. When Dave said, "Kim, you know I'm considering two different options on a topic," and then as an aside to Nick and me, "a topic I prefer to keep private." And then back to Kim, "You know the options, which is best?" and the glass went straight to 1 and Dave had his answer as well as his privacy.

After Dave and Nick got all their questions answered, there was a gap in the action and I jumped back in. "Kim," I said, "This is all amazing — please just amaze us more!" And she did immediately. The indicator spelled out 921FM, a radio station none of us had heard of. We went down the hall to Dave's room because he had the best stereo system with a radio tuner and the moment we tuned in 92.1 FM, For What It's Worth by Buffalo Springfield began. The great guitar lick intro was followed by Stephen Stills breaking in with

"There's something happening here. What it is ain't exactly clear."

Kim had delivered! "For What it's Worth" was not only one of my all-time favorite songs, but was also one that Nick and I had played a thousand times when we were in a band together. Because he knew how much I liked the song, he could attest to the fact that it was pretty amazing that it had started on the first harmonic pick of a guitar string that began a song with such a history for us. The other odd thing was that this song would be on any radio station at all since it was nearly twenty years old at the time.

I was now even more convinced that Kim had an incredible power and awareness of our lives. I decided to go all in with my next question. "Kim," I said, "what should I do with my life? I'm talking 'big picture' here? I mean I just moved to New York, but I feel like the qualities I value most in myself are least valued here." There was a pause, like Kim was thinking or allowing fellow spirits to weigh in on the topic. Then slowly, the glass spelled out LK956. This meant absolutely nothing to me. The first thing that came to mind was the LK Family Restaurant in Dayton, Ohio where I had lived when I was younger. But what would 956 mean?

Anyway, I thought we were back to gibberish and was ready to return to yes/no questions when Dave walked over to his bookshelf and produced a Bible. "Chris," he said, "are you aware that every book in The Bible has an abbreviation?" I was not. "Yes," explained Dave, "even the books with short names, like Mark or Luke have abbreviations … so, I'm looking up Luke 9, verses 5 and 6, since LK is the abbreviation for Luke.

Would you like to read it or shall I read it aloud?"

Dave read Luke 9:5-6 aloud, beginning with words of command from Jesus to his disciples: "'And wherever they do not receive you, when you leave that town shake off the dust from your feet as a testimony against them.' And they departed and went through the villages, preaching the gospel and healing everywhere."

I was stunned. Good stunned, but stunned. Everything about every word in these two verses resonated deeply within me. The resonation was such that it felt like listening to a song that you loved even if you weren't thinking of the lyrics or singing along. Dave re-read the passage and two words, "departed" and "healing" stood out so prominently, it was as if they had been injected into me.

The evening's messages from Kim could have ended here, but they didn't. And the two verses of scripture Dave had read were so perfect a response to my inquiry, I assumed the message was complete, but Dave calmly said, "Now let's check Luke 9:56 too" and after turning the page said "verse 56 is 'And they went on to another village.'" All minds were now blown — absolutely and entirely exploded! I'd already accepted the perfection of understanding Kim's message as simply Luke 9:5-6, but that Luke 9:56 basically repeated and reinforced the exact same message of healing and departure was almost too much magic and miracle for me to bear.

Perhaps Kim — and God — knew we all were beyond our usual limits, because after we'd set the Bible down and asked another question, the glass didn't budge. "She's gone," said Dave, speaking the truth that we already felt. Kim had left the room, without a goodbye, and our conversation with her concluded. What had not left the room, however, was our sense that God had been able to lovingly advise all of us through her.

When I got back to my apartment, I went to bed even though I felt wide awake. And I prayed, which was rare, and prayed out loud, which was never. But somehow it felt right after all our speaking aloud to Kim all night. I didn't use the word God much (lots of baggage!) but I said something like "Heavenly Being, who is AMAZING, thank you for Kim! Please surround all of her surviving relatives with love and peace and joy and comfort. Thank you for her life and for mine. Thank you for making the earth and heavens so intriguing! Oh, and also, if it's true that I'm going to live 50 or 60 more years, thanks very much for that since we both know that's more than I deserve!" After praying, and extinguishing my last cigarette for the night, I confess I said a few final words. "Goodnight, Kim," I whispered, "I love you."

When my lease expired five weeks later, I packed up my Datsun station wagon, left New York and slowly wandered my way down the highway until the road stopped in Key West, Florida. I don't know that I did any preaching there, but people said I was a good waiter and I got lots of songs written. Key West and I were a good match and I stayed there until it was time to go.

Abortion Healing

When I was 22 years old, I had an abortion. Of course I didn't physically have it, but the guilt I felt was so overwhelming, that I might as well have. And unlike most negative feelings I'd experienced, this guilt didn't fade with time but instead got bigger and more oppressive until I was unable to do anything except think about how terrible I was. When the guilt was reaching its peak, I even contemplated suicide, thinking it might be a "double win"; it would both end my intense pain and maybe appease God by demonstrating that I knew how horrible I was.

One irony in the whole debacle was that I was never anti-abortion, and was consistently, if only moderately, on the pro-choice side of the continuum. Friends of mine, male and female, had made the decision to abort accidental pregnancies, and I was a calm and supportive friend to them. I had been equally supportive of a woman I worked with at a bakery who decided to carry a baby full term and put it up for adoption.

The other odd thing about "my abortion" was that I could have excused myself from some of the responsibility. The woman with whom I got pregnant was officially my ex-girlfriend and we'd been broken up for three or four months without any contact of any kind. When we ran into each other at a bar all that time later, we were as attracted to one another as ever and within a few hours, we were passionately acting on that attraction. Just as I was lighting our post-passion cigarettes, she said in a sheepish voice, "We shouldn't have done that!" I assumed she meant that because we were no longer a couple, we should no longer be having sex. Wrong. Apparently, she had gone off the pill right after we had broken up. Since she had been on the pill when I met her, I had assumed that she had stayed on it after we were no longer together.

Anyway, the relationship didn't resume after that night but I found out six weeks later she was pregnant and I knew she was telling the truth when she told me it had to be my child. And strangely, it was something I'd known since the night we conceived.

Neither she nor I really considered the possibility of having and raising the child, as a married or unmarried couple, nor did she consider having the baby and putting it up for adoption. It's as if we both knew from the beginning that this baby would be aborted.

In the days before the abortion, I actually went to the library to read about it. What I learned was it was my job to be there for the pregnant woman as much as possible. So I decided to be as caring and attentive as I could be. And on the day of the abortion and for several days afterward, I was a back-rubbing, ice-pack-bringing, caring ex-boyfriend. On the surface, these actions looked like kindness, but I knew they were more motivated by guilt and distress than by genuine love or caring. I was "doing the right thing," but not for the right reasons, which probably made my ex-girlfriend feel even more burdened and alone.

All of which made my guilt even more unbearable. Instead of feeling relief, I was unable to do anything except think about how I was falling miles short of my own sense of morality and honor. My self-loathing simply had no limit and as hard as each day was, the next was invariably worse.

Finally, in total desperation, I phoned Jack, my closest friend back in Ohio. I confessed everything to him, including the fact that I was considering suicide both as a form of penitence and also just to make the pain stop. Jack listened very patiently, completely without judgment, and then said, "You know how our parents said — and in the church we always heard — all that 'Jesus died for our sins' stuff? Does thinking about that help?"

The funny thing is that Jack and I had never once discussed God or Jesus (even though three out of four of our parents were ordained ministers). But my friend's words were well timed. I was way too broken and burdened to have any energy left to spend on being too cool for God. As soon as we ended the phone call, I realized I already felt better. Why had I gone so long in secrecy without sharing my feelings with someone? I just sat there and reflected on my friend's wise words. Without even deciding to, the word Jesus began to roll around in my consciousness, and with each minute I could feel forgiveness and release. I didn't even actually ask for forgiveness, I just kept thinking the name "Jesus." I even said it out loud, finally, and added "please help."

It took a few weeks to really turn the corner and to begin accepting the forgiveness that was fully offered, but I did manage to make some progress. And progress was really important since it meant I no longer thought I should jump in front of the Amtrak train on its way to Detroit. An incidental lesson that I also learned during this period was that bourbon wasn't helping me cope as much as I thought it was; although it had pain-killing qualities, it was far more likely to intensify suicidal thoughts than reduce them. Alcohol was better suited for celebration than medication, at least for me anyway.

I know I was completely sober when about a month after Jack's and my conversation (and about six weeks after the abortion), I had the most extraordinarily happy dream of my life. In it I was holding the hand of a beautiful little girl — maybe two or three years old — with huge blue eyes and blond hair. We were standing near the entrance to the Cleveland Zoo, where I'd only been once when I was about two or three myself. In the dream I could feel the hand of the child so perfectly and she looked up at me with trust and love and power. Because I was absolutely positive at the age of 22 that I would never want a wife or kids in my lifetime, I just assumed that this little girl in my dreams was an angel that was bringing forgiveness, peace and calm to me.

I dreamed of her regularly for years. I never went more than two or three months without dreaming of the beautiful angel child. The image of that precious toddler brought me joy every time, and the timing of the dreams was also miraculous, often happening when I most needed a bit of affirmation from the universe.

Looking back on all of this, I know now that those dreams were full of invitation as well as affirmation, because nine years after the abortion, my daughter Maya Elizabeth was born. She had huge blue eyes and a head full of white-blonde hair was soon to follow. The child in my dreams had arrived.

When Maya was about two and a half, she was talking to her mother and me and said completely out of the blue, "Don't you two remember when I was up in the sky trying to get you together? I kept saying 'come on you guys, you two get together so I can be'" and even put her hands tightly together as she spoke.

I often say "there are no ifs in life" but if there were, I would say that IF it hadn't been for the abiding generosity of earth and heaven and for the incarnate beings of God — Jack, Jesus and Maya foremost among them — I never would have lived to be 23 years old, nor 33, which was my age when Maya and I walked hand in hand at the Cleveland Zoo.

Jesus' Birthday

Sometime in the mid-1990s, I began publishing a tiny hand-written newsletter called Talks With Jesus. Once a month, I'd stay up after my wife and daughters were asleep, and after praying and meditating, I'd imagine that I could talk with Jesus — privately, just us two — and what he would say. I'd then photocopy my hand-written notes and deliver them to anyone who wanted a copy; predictably, they were mostly friends willing to play along. Occasionally, I'd solicit questions for Jesus from readers when I'd run out of my own. Invariably, they were excellent, ranging from asking Jesus if he had liked sports (not particularly) to whether or not he'd had a girlfriend when he was younger (yes).

But the most life-changing event came from a question that, at first, didn't strike me as all that important — a friend asked about Jesus' astrological sign. So, on that friend's behalf late one evening, I asked Jesus about it. "Jesus, there's a song by Jerry Jeff Walker called 'Jesus was a Capricorn' [since December 25 is in Capricorn].

Is that true or were you actually something else?" Jesus said, "Something else" and after a pause (Jesus loves pauses), he added, "I was a Libra." I said, "When is that?" and he said, "Look it up." Jesus often said "look it up." He never ever answered a question that could be looked up easily. So I did look up the dates (Libra is late September to late October), and then said, "OK, we got the month range, what is the actual day?" And as Jesus would often do, he replied with total perfect silence. I asked again a little more forcefully (more silence), and then asked why he wouldn't share something that wouldn't hurt me to know. At the moment I asked that, I realized there was actually something unhealthy in my curiosity about the topic, and that these epiphanies often happened in the silences where I was hoping to get spoken answers from Jesus. That said, I couldn't stop thinking about it. And I'd re-ask every now and then, pretty much knowing that I wasn't going to get the answer, obsessed with knowing the answer to a question that a friend had originally asked and I hadn't been curious about at all.

So now that I knew I was being obsessive about the real date of Jesus' birth, I asked myself why I was that way. What I discovered was that I had a deep — and nearly life-long — resentment of Christmas, with lots of unacknowledged or buried hurts from holidays when I was young. Christmases had been overshadowed by my father's excessive frugality and both my parents' illusions and silly hopes about having Norman Rockwell holidays without being willing to look bravely at the level of dysfunction in our household. I looked at all these things and realized that although my wife had planned and prepared six or seven years of extraordinary Christmases for me and our two daughters, I still had more than 30 years of anti-Christmas baggage and unhealed thoughts about the season. I realized I could be more grateful to my wife for healing Christmases for me and that I could prayerfully extend some of those good wishes to my parents, whose house neither my two sisters nor I had been to for Christmas in ages.

And in all this rumination, I completely forgot Jesus. I completely forgot needing to know with obsessive-compulsive exactitude what his birthday was if we extended the Gregorian calendar back to 4 BC or 6 BC or whatever it was. My Christmas healing made my curiosity about the exact date of Jesus' birthday disappear altogether. And none of the readers of Talks With Jesus seemed to be clamoring for an exact date either.

Many months later, during the week after Thanksgiving, my neighbor across the street was putting up his Christmas tree lights very early, as was his tradition. There was absolutely nothing exceptional about the few strings of lights he put up every year so I have no idea what made me look out the window that afternoon. But when I did, I saw a man on our side of the street, standing on our sidewalk and leaning back on our cyclone fence so that his head was actually over our yard. It was as if he needed an extra few feet of distance to get the best view of the neighbor's lights even though he was more than 100 feet away from my neighbor's house. It seemed unlikely that an extra foot would give him that much more of an improved perspective. I was taken by how utterly focused he was on the Christmas lights and at a certain point I just said, "Hi."

There was nothing threatening about the man so there was nothing accusing in my tone like when people say "may I help you" when what they really mean is "will you get the hell off my property" or "do I need to call the police?" As he turned to look at me, I had this feeling that he already knew I was standing there—in fact, somehow knew when I had left the kitchen 30 seconds earlier. His eyes were unlike eyes I've ever seen, huge and dark, and way far apart on each side of his nose bridge. He looked directly at me and s-l-o-w-l-y said hello back. To say that this man was "different" would be THE understatement of my entire life. He had long hair, more black than brown, and his skin color was what I imagine skin would be if one could average out the skin color of all 8 billion people on the planet.

Eventually I said, "Excuse me, do you mind if I ask what you're doing?" Again, without accusation but with true curiosity. He said "I'm looking at those Christmas lights—checking to see that they're balanced." He looked back at the lights and said, "Balance is really important [long pause] for a Libra" and turned again to look right at me. The huge eyes smiled at me. From this point on, it felt as if I were performing a script that had been written long before and that I had memorized for this day's "play." So I said, "So you're a Libra," which produced a very slow nod of his head and a "yes." We were both savoring this simple conversation. I even managed a dramatic pause myself before asking, "Would you mind if I asked the exact day of your birthday?" "Libra-man" exhaled and looked like he genuinely was having fun. Again he stared right at me with eyes that were hugely bemused and deeply loving, and said, "October....11."

It's amazing sometimes how un-miraculous a miracle can feel! With an ease that almost never happens between any two people, we stared at each other in silence a long time before I finally said thank you for sharing that date and for the more valuable invitation to achieve greater balance. One of the things my obsession with finding out Jesus' birthday had taught me was that my Christmas joy in the present and Christmas unhappiness from the past were creating a huge imbalance in my life. A gift that God certainly wanted me to receive was balance and to let God birth in me a deeper understanding, and greater forgiveness, of my past.

Those who know how these things work will correctly guess that my conversation with this unusual man was a once-in-a-lifetime experience. I neither expected to see him again nor hoped I would. Although my neighbors would hang their lights every year at almost the identical time, I never looked to see if a Libra, whose specialty was "balance," was standing on my sidewalk. In fact, within a few years of that day, my family and I moved away from that house and Key West and all the physical reminders of that day.

Spiritual reminders abound, however, and I cherish this person's presence frequently. And, predictably, I still talk with Jesus in conversations that continue to go best after prayer and meditation, celebrating him especially on October 11, and balancing that with the other celebration on his Capricorn birthday in late December.

Postscript:

When I attended seminary, I discovered that there was absolutely uniform agreement among scholars that the biblical line "shepherds keeping their flocks by night" ensured that Jesus' birth could only have occurred in very late summer or fall, because to this day, that is the only time when shepherds spend their nights in the fields around Bethlehem. Those who make an educated guess often choose late September and early October (Libra days) as the most likely range for Jesus' birthdate. Also, the majority of scholars think Jesus would be older than the calendar year because of fairly accurate records of Roman politicians. My personal practice is to give gratitude for a Jesus who is five years ahead of our Western calendar, which would mean he was born in 6 BCE (Before Common Era), since 0 does not count as a year. When I wrote in my daytime planner, "Happy Birthday, Jesus — 2005 years old!" on October 11, 2000, and drew a huge heart around it, a still small voice said, "Balance!"

Carole Gerbracht Dies
January 9, 1992 - June 10, 1997

Anybody who's ever spent time in a city has likely witnessed a guy who walks alone down the sidewalk — or even the middle of the street — screaming something angry, resentful or accusatory that never ends. For 38 years when I'd see people like that, I'd always feel a little sorry for them, but, to be totally honest, I would also think something like, "Thank God I'm not that crazy loser!" And I'd think it without any sense of irony that my judgment made me a bigger loser than any of the screamers. But as proof that those who judge also get judged, on one afternoon in June of 1997, I became that guy walking down the street raging non-stop to earth and heaven: Hearing that five-year-old Carole Gerbracht had died while playing hide-and-seek so enraged me that I couldn't hold still and I couldn't keep quiet.

    I was pissed off not only that Carole was dead, but I was pissed off by how she died. While Carole was looking for a great hiding place, plywood hurricane shutters had shifted and fallen on her, breaking her neck instantly and leaving her eight-year-old sister Claudia to discover

Carole's limp body moments later. I had witnessed miraculous events in life where the only possible explanation was supernatural or divine intervention. If divine intervention existed, and I was absolutely positive it did, why hadn't it been on duty that morning?

And why had this happened just three weeks after Carole's parents, Jim and Adele, had decided to become members of Peace Covenant Presbyterian Church, a loving little corner of Christendom that also hosted the Key West Pre-School Co-op where we all taught and cared for our children, including five-year-old Carole?

And what was with God's allowing the cause of the fatality to be from materials that Jim Gerbracht had proactively gathered to protect his home and the kind and loving family that lived in it? The irony of that somehow multiplied the "tragic-factor" and made the most awful possible situation, worse.

And how would this tragic death affect Carole's grandmother, Helen, the Gerbracht with whom I was closest? Helen, like me, was known as a person who was so "into God" that some people considered us a bit off. I knew Helen as a saint, however, and knew that she had already buried a husband and cared her whole life for a daughter who had mental-health challenges. Why would God allow such a tragic thing to happen to someone as good as Helen? At seventy-something years old, Helen would likely have asked God why she couldn't have died instead of her son's daughter. What was I going to say to her when she called the next evening with names for the prayer-chain – the same phone-prayer chain that she'd launched and recruited me to join? Or would she even bother to call?

I mean the idea of adding "the Gerbracht family" to the prayer list seemed like an exercise in futility.
Yeah, I'd pray all right, if by "pray" we mean "talking to God," because I already had PLENTY to say to God regarding the Gerbracht family. No need to wait for the names to show up on a prayer-chain list.

How I envied atheists that day! Believing in nothing except the randomness of life would have spared me the rage that I felt toward God. My faith in God was a burden in another way that day, as well, because I had a bit of a pastoral reputation. I belonged to three different churches (including Peace Covenant Presbyterian), sang in two church choirs, and also regularly provided intensive healing-prayer sessions in my free time.

And within an hour of Carole's accident, my phone was ringing non-stop. The people calling, mostly parents and fellow board members from the pre-school co-op, were as confused and in shock as I was, but I felt like there was an expectation from some of them that I would somehow be able to say something that would make sense of the whole situation. If there was a magic phrase that would comfort and heal everyone, myself included, I didn't know it. Probably the wisest thing I did was to not talk much at all and let people tell their story — how they heard the news, who told them, where they were when they heard it and how sad they were.

But the more I listened, the angrier I got. Not at the people on the phone, but at God. As people phoned all afternoon, they usually updated me on whatever news they'd heard about the Gerbrachts. And I guess as a coping mechanism, the hope that Carole might somehow be resuscitated started getting passed around the phone chain. Carole's neck was broken, they said, but she had been taken to the hospital and doctors were trying everything, including extreme, super-invasive measures, to revive her. I even allowed myself to hope with them for a while. I remember walking into our front yard and taking a big breath of warm tropical summer air and thinking the phrase, "Peace. Be still." The masters, like Lao Tzu or Jesus, could always be at peace, and I'm going to do the same, I said to myself. I even started hoping that "reports of Carole's death had been exaggerated." And for a couple hours, I felt a lot better as I clung to this hope.

    The phone even stopped ringing for a time until Brenda, a close friend of the Gerbrachts, phoned and let me know that Carole had been pronounced dead by the doctors.

    I began to tell myself that I'd already known that anyway, and that I'd known that my hope was silly, but truthfully, it felt like Carole had died a second time that day — like God had let her die twice.

    And it was then that I snapped and my anger took over entirely. My rage went from zero to sixty in an instant. My fists were clenched, my jaw was tight and rather than breathing, I was huffing and puffing and looking for a house to blow down. I could not think, I could not hear, I was pure rage and out on the street, speed walking and swearing at earth and heaven, but mainly heaven.

    If you think swearing is a craft perfected by drunks and sailors, you should have heard me that night — and I've never served in the Armed Forces and was sober as black coffee.

And just like the crazy angry men swearing their way down the street, I didn't really have much to say. In fact, if someone had removed all the swear words and summarized the themes that I repeated for two hours, it could all have been said in a few words: God, I'm super-angry and it's all Your fault!

But some things can't be summarized — I needed to live the longer version that day.

I was like a guy with a plastic pail and beach shovel, threatening a mountain, promising to make it a valley! I challenged God to appear so that I could beat Him up in a fight and feed his blanking body parts to the drug dealer's dog on Flagler Ave. I am grateful to this day that no one called the police because my rage might have been uncontainable and might even have spilled over onto the responding officer, if one had come to investigate the loud lunatic disturbing an otherwise quiet Tuesday evening. Looking back on it, I'm sure God must have been watching over me with love the entire time I was spewing hateful shit toward Him — it's like God knew I'd run out of gas on my own without having to go to jail for the night to simmer down.

By the time I did get home a couple hours later, I was entirely spent. I flopped onto the sofa and kicked off my flip-flops. Before my brain had time to recharge enough to break into more ranting, I felt as if a strong, warm, gigantic King-Kong-size hand gently began to wrap itself around me, in effect, replacing the couch. And instantly, I heard these exact words spoken more clearly than if a human had walked into the room to say them. "Since you're so fond of the word, consider you don't know shit."

It's as if God had been patiently waiting two hours for me to shut up so the record could be set straight in one clear sentence!

And in an instant, I had a bunch of thoughts: Was that God who just rebuked and humbled me? Did God actually say "shit?" Is that even allowed? There's an expression that says, "When God gets involved, we're usually brought up short." It hadn't crossed my mind for hours that I was anything other than totally right about everything. But everything I'd "known" was making me miserable so the suggestion that I was clueless, or a guy who didn't "know shit," actually relieved me of the burden of my own certitude. And for the first time all day, I grinned, and pretty soon I was chuckling, and then full-on laughing at the impossibility of it all. I was laughing so hard that I had to stifle it so I wouldn't wake my one-year-old, Sophia, or slow her down from falling asleep, but it all was so strangely funny I couldn't stop. And as I quieted myself down a bit, I realized I wasn't laughing anymore, but crying, just like someone had pulled back the "funny" fader bar in a recording studio while pushing the "sadness" fader bar up. Tears I'd been holding back all afternoon and evening now began flowing and soon turned to sobbing.

Although I had just muttered and sputtered hatred all over the neighborhood for half the evening, I was self-conscious about my tears, so to give myself privacy, I walked out to the carport, got into our station wagon and cried harder than I ever had before. Something I learned that night was that if I cry really hard, I don't have to cry long. The tears subsided fairly quickly and after wiping my face and hands with the McDonald's napkins that were in the console, I felt a thousand percent better. I looked out the window and saw the waxing crescent moon that I had not noticed at all earlier. Although that would not have been a big deal for some people, it was a huge indicator of how "off" I had been earlier, because I have been a moon-watcher all my life, and always know what phase the moon is in and where and when it is visible. In my rage, I had not noticed it once although it had been directly overhead the whole time. I climbed out of the car and started walking again, this time as silent as that moon — its brightness undergirded by a giant band of cumulous clouds to the south.

About a quarter mile down the road, I turned back in to the residential neighborhood to the east of my house and realized I was close to Helen Gerbracht's house. I'd like to say that going to Helen's was my idea, but truthfully, I know I was nudged there by a Power more empathetic and caring than I was. And a power that wasn't as handcuffed by propriety, since it was at least 10 or 10:30 p.m. by now and I hadn't called first.

When I arrived at Helen's, she greeted me with a hug and said, "How kind of you to come by." Helen was so kind and warm and generous that I actually knew that I didn't need to apologize for not phoning first, but I did anyway because I knew my mom would haunt me in my dreams if I didn't!

Helen was always a woman who could say a lot in a little but she seemed to understand that even if she didn't need to talk, I needed to hear her voice. "We lost Carole," she said as she presented a framed photo of her two granddaughters. Carole was in the foreground and her older sister Claudia was behind her. To say that the photo striking would be a huge understatement. Carole stared right into the camera with an intensity and power that was astonishing. Precocious didn't even begin to describe her look; this was clearly a self-possessed child who was the master of her own destiny. Claudia, by contrast, looked like me in all my childhood photos — a standard-issue kid captured at a random moment. But Carole stared straight into the camera lens — and now, stared straight from the picture frame into Helen's and my eyes — and her expression said, "Don't even dare to think that I'm dead and gone, because you both know better!"

Helen produced another photo, this one of Carole alone, but her intense stare straight down the barrel of the camera was almost identical — powerful, clear and precocious by decades. Although it was a medical/physical fact that Carole had died hours earlier, her eyes in the photo said something else. "Get with the TRUE program, you!" those eyes commanded, and I felt humbled by her power gaze.

"It's almost as if Carole knew when these photos were taken that someday broken-hearted people would be looking at them," I said to Helen. Helen put her hand on my arm, the one holding the photo, and gave it a little rub. "She's very special," she said as we gazed together at Carole the Super Child. For a millionth of a second, I wondered if Carole was such a rare and wonderful soul that she only needed five and a half years on earth to do everything that needed to be done — to learn what she needed to learn and teach what she needed to teach. Could that possibly be right?

A long silence followed. Very long.

"I was so angry when I heard the news that I told God that I was going to rip Him a second asshole," I confessed to Helen as if she were a priest who could absolve me.

"Did God respond?"

"When I finally shut up, yes," I said.

Helen raised her eyebrows in a wordless "And...?"

"God said that since I'm so fond of the word, I should consider I don't know shit!"

Helen smiled and started to nod her head slowly. "That sounds like God!" she mused.

"Doesn't it? And God must have known that I would have had a heart attack if He'd used the F-word!"

We laughed some more and once again, tears came. But this time, the tears were from laughing, and miraculously, for joy.

Then Helen said something important. "Carole's death must have really frightened you ... since you have two young daughters, too."

Boom! Helen was so wise that she understood me better than I understood myself. I hadn't even asked myself why I'd been so angry and now I realized that it was all based on fear. I thought my anger was akin to self-righteous indignation, and that expressing that anger was right and powerful. But Helen kindly guided me to see that all my actions were based on fear; I was "frightened," terrified even, and resented God for all the ways that I couldn't control every detail of the protection of my family.

I was also projecting lots of my feelings onto Carole's dad, Jim, and feeling imagined rage on his behalf. In all my screaming at God, I hadn't once gotten over myself enough to pray that God give Jim Gerbracht peace and strength and to comfort him and his family in their mourning.

    Powerful forces were coming to my aid even though I'd neither asked for them nor felt I needed them. First, God let me know I didn't know shit, and then Helen invited me to see that I was scared shitless. And Carole implored me, via her photos, to be wiser, stronger and truer — basically, to get my shit together. There was lots to think and pray about before the funeral; and a lifetime's worth of Crazy God Shit to process, something I would only be able to do with the help of insane Grace and Love.

Carole Gerbracht's Funeral

As frightening as "hurricane season" sounded to me when I first heard the term, I quickly learned that summers in semi-tropical environments are the quietest time of the year. Although the official dates of hurricane season in the Florida Keys (and the entire North Atlantic Ocean) are June 1 to November 30, people in the areas affected by the storms know that almost all of the "big ones" occur in August and September. But the typical day for most of hurricane season is still and hot; each lazy day follows another and even the rain, which is frequent, is usually gentle.

June 1997 would have been a month of those typically quiet days in Key West, the kind of month no one remembers years later, had it not been for Carole Gerbracht's death. That she was killed by a leaning stack of hurricane shutters that fell on her while she played hide-and-seek made her death an event that affected everyone. Even those who didn't know the Gerbrachts knew that it could have happened to them, since most households had a similar stack of wood somewhere in the yard or garage.

Although the weather hadn't changed with Carole's death, the quiet of summer was completely gone. Along with the sadness everyone felt for the Gerbrachts, we'd all lost our sense of safety. Between Carole's death on Tuesday and her funeral on Friday, I wasn't in a single conversation that didn't include a mention of the tragedy. After discussing Carole and sharing the date and time of her funeral, there would often be talk about efforts to make our homes safer for small children. Parents did walk-throughs of their entire properties, inside and out, checking for anything that might be too heavy, sharp or poisonous. We reminded each other to make sure that kitchen cupboard doors had safety latches and that heavy bookshelves were bolted to the wall. One mom said to me, "Hearing about Carole made me feel SO helpless — the only thing I could do to make myself feel safer was to finally enroll my twins in a 'learn to swim' class! I feel so silly, but more, I feel sad."

I actually envied this mother. She was so aware of her feelings and totally open about sharing them. I was embarrassed about mine and kept them hidden, because even though my mind and soul told me it was unwise and unhealthy, I was still unable to totally lay my anger down and give it up to God for transformation.

So I was angry that Carole had died, and ashamed that I was angry, and stuck in an endless loop of thoughts that fed the anger, which produced more shame. And I held those feelings all week and carried them with me to the outdoor venue where Carole's funeral was held.

Although the Gerbrachts had just joined the local Presbyterian church, there was never any discussion about having the funeral in the 200-seat sanctuary of the Church. Instead, the Gerbrachts and Rev. Pat Ashford chose the West Martello Tower — a pre-Civil War fort turned into a public garden — and coupled that choice with a huge "spread-the-word" campaign that everyone with folding chairs should bring them to augment all the folding chairs from the church.

Bettina, our daughters and I arrived with collapsible chairs, and immediately saw Carole's mom, Adele. I was taken off guard. I guess I assumed that a huge percentage of the 1,500 people who showed up would want to offer a loving or consoling word to her before (or after) the service and that there would be a line or a group around the family at all times, similar to visitations at funeral homes. But there she was, crossing a street alone when we bumped into her. Although I actually knew Adele better than my wife did since I was the primary parent at the Key West Pre-School Co-op, I was mostly silent after managing a quick "I'm so sorry, Adele."

Bettina's and her conversation was of mothers, by mothers and for mothers, and I ached as I listened. I remember Adele saying that she knew Carole's spirit was still "alive" somewhere, somehow, but that there was a longing in her arms to give Carole "hugs that only a mother can give. My arms miss her the most."

My wife was usually the person you wanted around at difficult or stressful moments but she set a personal record that day. Bettina grew up in northern Germany and, at the risk of stereotyping, had a tough side that almost bordered on hard-assed-ness. But when her protective power mixed with caring and love, she was something to behold. With the perfect blend of strength and respect, concern and love, she took Adele in her arms and held her, and for those moments, Bettina had enough strength for both of them.

And adding to the love magic, Sophia, our one-year-old, did what she had never done before. As Adele and Bettina's hug was concluding, Sophia motioned from the papoose carrier on my chest that she wanted to go to Adele. "I think Sophia wants to come to you," I said to Adele, not entirely sure that she'd have the time or desire. Truthfully, it had made me feel a bit self-conscious that I was standing there with my two living, healthy daughters and that Adele now only had one, so I was relieved when Adele smiled at Sophia and gently took her and cuddled her. "Ahhh, babies!" Adele said to Bettina with an "only women really get it" look.

By now, a bit of a crowd had gathered and we excused ourselves. The Gerbrachts had decided on an open casket for Carole and the viewing time was before the service. I headed that way alone since Bettina and the girls had decided not to join me for a moment with Carole's body before the casket was shut.

I know that opinions vary widely on open viewings, but for me they are far more healing than they are traumatic. Carole's casket was near an old stone wall — the fort's boundary — and beyond the wall to the south stretched light green Caribbean water for as far as one could see until the water merged at the distant horizon with thick, tropical summer clouds. With this magnificent panorama as a backdrop, I stood by Carole's casket and prayed for her, her family, my family and the whole world.

I looked a long time at the many visible scrapes and bruises around Carole's neck; the man or woman who prepared Carole's body for viewing could easily have hidden these blue, purple and black marks under a thick skin-colored base but had chosen not to. And this may sound corny, or worse, stupid, but while I was looking at the injuries on Carole's neck, a thought came to me that took me by surprise: "I'm looking at Jesus."

And instantly, I was praying again. "God," I thought silently, "I don't actually think Carole is going to sit up in this coffin and then climb out and go hug Adele, but I am proclaiming her resurrection anyway. I don't know what I'm asking for, but I'm asking You to resurrect this whole thing, whatever that means!"

What I didn't know then is that resurrection comes in a lot of different ways and at all different speeds. The first hint of resurrection I felt came soon after the service started. Rev. Pat Ashford had chosen two Psalms that she read before her eulogy. The first, Psalm 23 (the one that starts with "The Lord is my shepherd"), was to be expected, but then she read Psalm 131, which took me by surprise. The surprise wasn't in the fact that she chose a very rare Psalm that is almost never heard at a funeral, but instead, by the sensations the words caused in me.

For the entire 20 or 30 seconds that Rev. Pat read the Psalm, I felt like I was "becoming" the Psalm and it was somehow "absorbing" me. I had heard people say things like they were "fed" by God's Word, whether it was Torah, or The Bible or The Koran or some other sacred text, but I always heard it as a metaphor rather than a literal sensation. But before Rev. Pat had finished the very first verse (My heart is not proud, LORD, my eyes are not haughty; I do not concern myself with great matters or things too wonderful for me), I had this sense that my mind, soul and body were being stuffed with things that were good, true and beautiful — and miraculously ALIVE! I was literally being fed by holy writing.

And it didn't escape my attention that Psalm 131 repeated a pledge I'd just made moments earlier while viewing Carole's body, namely, that I'd given up on trying to make complete sense of Carole's death. But, like the writer of the Psalm, I did actually believe that God could somehow make wonderful things happen in the middle of all this pain and grief. I had decided to "quiet myself like a weaned child" and "put [my] hope in the LORD both now and forever," just as the verses of Psalm 131 suggested I should.

Rev. Pat's eulogy was a continuation of the same Grace that was covering the entire funeral and everyone there. All these years later, I still remember the first word of her message. Pat walked to the microphone, and after a long silence said, "Unfathomable."

Which was followed by more silence.

Carole's death five days earlier was absolutely "unfathomable," but Pat knew that all 1,500 of us attending the funeral had spent all week trying to fathom it anyway — to make sense of the sensless and to find love in the loss.

After acknowledging that loss, Pat continued with a remembrance of the weather on the day Carole died. She had driven through rain on US Route 1 southwest of Miami and the first rays of sun were visible through thick clouds as she approached Key West. It was a simple and solid message with God's power and healing being represented by brilliant sunlight, but Pat had done a "weather report" sermon for a larger and more miraculous reason.

After her eulogy ended, Carole's older sister Claudia came to the microphone to speak. To this day, if I ever need to be inspired by a memory of courage, I picture eight-year-old Claudia speaking softly to the huge crowd at her own sister's funeral.

"After we left the hospital," Claudia began, "we decided to stop at the beach on our way home and watch the sunset. While we stood on the beach, I looked at the sky and right above the clouds, I could see Carole. She told me not to be sad and that she loved everyone and that she was not sad about anything. I wanted to tell you that."

Claudia's words spread through the congregation like a healing balm. So many people were crying that the sniffling and nose-blowing were audible as Claudia shared her vision of a peaceful and loving Carole, who was changed by death, but not eliminated by it. It made such perfect sense that Carole would "appear" to her sister first. Claudia and she were playing hide-and-seek together when she died and Claudia was the one who discovered her under the plywood.

Then God provided a bit of comic relief. I know others might think that what happened next was a random event, but I still see it as divine all these years later. When Claudia had finished speaking, a woman who no one knew came over to the microphone and introduced herself. She had one of those New Age names that women often adopted in the 1990s like Summer Dawn or Serenity Sunrise.

After she said her name, it was clear that she didn't know Carole, or any of the Gerbrachts, or a single person at the funeral, but was a tourist who was just happening by and liked the idea of getting up to talk.

"I didn't know the person you lost, but my spirit guide tells me that she was a special person," she began, and then acted like she was listening to that guide. "Yes, yes, a very special soul, so I wish I could have met her." My hunch is that "Serenity" knew she was bombing, so she abruptly switched her style to "vamp-sexy." She actually lifted a little finger to her lips and with a breathier Marilyn Monroe voice said, "Thank you! And peace to you today," and she wiggle-walked away from the microphone. It's not that I doubted that she had a "spirit guide," but I don't think the guide had mentioned that her biggest gift to the group was unintended humor. Even my six-year-old, Maya, had a puzzled look on her face and after she whispered something to Bettina, I could see Bettina was suppressing a laugh.

"Thank you," said the inscrutable Rev. Pat as Serenity walked away. God, she was a great pastor — on top of all her other skills, she was a good, and kind, actor! A singer got up to lead us in Amazing Grace and after that, Rev. Pat gave a final blessing and the service was over.

They say the three biggest reasons to have a funeral are 1) to acknowledge that the person has died, 2) to support the family of the deceased and 3) to mourn as a group. The Key West community had just done all three about as well as they could be done, given the difficulty of the circumstances.

And on a personal level, I'd gone the whole hour without once feeling any of the anger, confusion, blame and shame that had haunted me all week. Adele, Rev. Pat, Claudia and yes, even Serenity, had blessed me with a lightness I hadn't felt since Carole's death.

When the service was over, moms and kids hung out in little groups while many of the dads busied themselves with loading chairs onto the one flatbed and a few other pickup trucks. After helping out a bit with gathering and loading the folding chairs, I went to get our car while Bettina talked with other families. Within the first 100 yards, I bumped into Rev. Pat loading her things into her Ford Escort.

"Pat," I began, not knowing what I was going to say. "That service was really powerful ... no, that's not the word I want. It was 'lighten-ing.' Thank you!"

She paused and said, slowly, "Thank you!" Another pause. "Funerals only go well if you spend time aligning yourself with all the loving forces of heaven as you prepare for them. I suspect you'll be good at them!"

I stood there, blankly, pondering the clear implication of what she'd just said. Pat knew what Bettina and I did for a living, and officiating at funerals wasn't something I saw myself doing, ever; it was hard enough for me to even attend one.

"Don't panic, Chris," she added, "The voice from the clouds knows what's best."

Carole Victorious!

Life did, and did not, return to normal after Carole Gerbracht's funeral.

And that felt as right as it could and is probably how it is supposed to work. There's a healthy side to not attempting to return to one's pre-tragedy life as if nothing happened. It's as if people understood that a five-year-old's death should never be normalized with a "whatever happens, happens" passivity.

I'm sure everyone dealt with the Gerbrachts differently afterward. I never saw Adele, Jim or Claudia again without being a bit aware of the fact that they had buried a young child whom they loved and who loved them. Often, as my wife Bettina and our two daughters were doing something, I'd remember out of the blue that the Gerbrachts had been a family of four like we were, but now were three.

One lie that I mostly believed was that this tragedy was the reason I had been grumpy lately. At best, that was a half-truth, or maybe a quarter-truth. The primary reason for my grumpiness was actually Rev. Pat Ashford's "prophecy" that I would lead funerals, which I took to mean that I would be a pastor someday. I'd thought of that about a hundred times a day since she said it as we were leaving the place where Carole's funeral had been. Sure, I knew a cool clergy-person or two – especially Rev. Pat herself – but these were exceptions to a rule in my mind.

Under NO condition would I ever choose a career that attracted such a high percentage of self-righteous dorks, I promised myself with a self-righteous and dorky resolve.

If I'd been a better husband (and better man), I'd have shared my truest feelings with Bettina and admitted to myself and her that what Pat said had really shattered my status quo. And with a bit more self-appraisal, I would have discovered that my vulnerability to Pat's "prophecy" was heightened by the emotional exhaustion caused by Carole's death a few weeks earlier.

Rather than choose any of those wise and mature options, I griped about things that weren't the cause of my unsettledness.

One evening after our daughters were asleep and I was prepping shirts for the next day's production, I got in a mood to gripe. "Don't you ever get annoyed by how repetitive our business is?" I asked Bettina. "Every day it's the same thing, year after year after year."

This wasn't the first time that I had whined about how our painted-clothing business had become too routine. I knew I was being ridiculous; we lived in one of the premiere resort destinations in the world. Our business was so successful that we often double or triple paid our mortgage just because we could.

We worked as hard as we wanted and whenever we wanted. We were our own bosses. Our children spent hours every week on the beach at the most "Caribbean" jewel of the Florida State Park system, Fort Zachary Taylor.

Bettina had heard my griping before, but this time she responded with a different approach. "What if starting right now, we continued to make exactly the same income, but you didn't have to spend a minute earning it?" she asked. "What would you do if you were completely free to do whatever you wanted?"

This was not the first time that I had benefitted from Bettina's creative, calm approach to handling one of my "bitch and moan" moods, but this was her best response ever. The moment I put myself into this hypothetical world, I began to feel happier.

"Well," I began, "I'd go to the beach with you and the girls WAY more often. And I'd walk more, for exercise, but even more as a walking meditation, and I would sing to Sophia if I had the stroller and she was awake and I'd pray when she was sleeping. What else…I'd never miss another Bible class that Pat Ashford taught. And I'd certainly read the Bhagavad Gita (the holy book of Hinduism) faster — I've had it for two months and I've read maybe twenty pages! Oh, and Laura and Mike are trying to build up that contemporary service on Sunday afternoons at the Methodist church on Fleming Street — I'd probably switch to doing that two or three times a month instead of two or three times a year."

Living in Bettina's hypothetical "full income with no work" world was putting me in a better mood by the second – when I woke up from my "do whatever I want" daydream, she had the oddest expression on her face.

"What's that look?" I asked.

"I guess the look on my face is what happens when a woman realizes her husband is becoming a minister…"

And just as fast as my good mood had arrived, it was now gone. I confessed to Bettina that Pat Ashford had said the same thing and then I wasted fifteen minutes of Bettina's, and my own, time explaining why I would never ever be a minister, pastor or any kind of reverend, thank you very much.

When that ridiculous topic was settled and closed and put to rest, forever, never to be seriously discussed again, I was suddenly exhausted. Although I normally stayed up much later, I excused myself, went straight to bed and fell asleep instantly.

And in that sleep, Carole Gerbracht, the five-year-old girl who had died two weeks earlier, spoke to me. I say that she spoke, rather than "appeared" to me because this dream only had a soundtrack and no video. There was no burning bush or talking donkey like in a Bible story. Just like listening to music in complete darkness or with your eyes shut, helps you to hear it better, I could hear nothing but Carole and, eerily enough, I heard her perfectly — more clearly and memorably than any conversation with a living person, day or night.

The conversation didn't begin the usual way. Carole didn't say "Good morning, Chris, it's me Carole Gerbracht — yeah I know I'm dead but I can still communicate." And I didn't say, "Wow, this is cool, I'm talking to a ghost." And Carole didn't need to say "Don't be afraid" like angels in the Bible because she already knew I wasn't. And I knew that she knew that I had been to her funeral and that at that funeral her sister Claudia had shared a story of Carole's talking to her from above the clouds. Carole also knew that although not everyone had believed Claudia's report, I had TOTALLY believed it.

"I have a message for you to deliver for me," said Carole, getting right to business. "Tell my dad to tell my mom that I am holding her with arms of love."

Even in my dream, I was stunned and hesitant. Argumentative, too. "Whoa," I protested, "this doesn't make sense for a lot of reasons. First, why don't you just tell your mom yourself? And if you have to have me as the messenger, why wouldn't I just tell your mom directly, since I know your mom reasonably well and I don't know your dad at all?"

"When you tell my dad, you'll get the message just right, and he will tell my mom," said Carole, completely ignoring what I thought had been valid objections. Carole was no longer the little girl who had shyly given my older daughter and me one flower each one afternoon at the pre-school co-op. She had authority and spoke to me with a prophet's firmness.

"I love my parents equally," Carole continued, "but my concern for my mother is greater. Similar to how you are with your parents right now."

I knew that Carole had never met my parents, but since she knew this exact detail about my present feelings toward them, I assumed that she pretty much knew everything. But she clearly didn't know everything, or she would have known this fact, too: that I was not, under any circumstance, going to phone her dad, or anyone else I didn't know at all, to tell them that I had just spoken with their dead daughter and that the same dead daughter had given me a message to deliver. She had to know this, but I wanted to re-confirm my refusal.

"Carole, I am unwilling to deliver your message," I began, but as I "dream-spoke," I realized she was no longer there. Spirit-Carole had taken her wise, loving and bossy self away and left me alone. My complaining refusal had gone unheard.

The conversation was over and I was on my own. I sat up in bed, wide awake, and actually said aloud to myself, "Huh, I guess dying makes you smarter … and way more authoritative!"

I glanced to my left and saw that our one-year-old, Sophia, was sound asleep in our bed and that Bettina was looking at me with half-open eyes. "Are you talking to me?" she asked.

"No, sorry," I said softly, "I'm not talking to anyone," and then whispered just in case Carole could still hear me, "especially Jim Gerbracht!"

The next morning, I told Bettina about my "conversation" with Carole, and made a huge self-drama out of the fact that I felt Carole had put me in a lose-lose position: If I didn't talk to Jim, Carole would be angry, or worse, haunt me forever in my sleep; and if I did tell Jim, he'd likely accuse me of insanity, or cruelty, or both.

"Well, if it really was Carole, she'll make a way for you," Bettina said. "And if it turns out it wasn't Carole but just a weird dream, you'll be wise to do nothing and let it pass. It's a win-win, actually."

The next night, Carole visited again just like she had the first time, in a dream that was super-real and unforgettable. And again, "audio only."

"Your worrying, like fear, is always unproductive," said Carole. "When you speak with my dad, the timing will be perfect. That's how it is when the message is love, because even now, I am holding my mom with arms of love."

Even in my dream state, I paused to think about whether love is always perfectly timed. I wanted to disprove it so I could convince Carole that she needed to deliver the message herself, to either her dad or mom, but to leave me out of it. But before I could come up with a reply, I realized that once again, she had already departed.

When I woke the next morning, the only thing I remembered was Carole's message. Nothing about calling or contacting Jim felt like "perfect timing," so I just let the topic go and relaxed.

And I had a great day. I thought about Carole's phrase "when the message is love" and how I could be more loving in my life, and when, where, and with whom. The day's work was practically effortless and all was well with the world.

That evening, I got a call from Helen Gerbracht, Carole's grandmother and Jim's mother. That Helen called wasn't unusual at all because she called twice a week to give me names for a telephone prayer-chain that she led. What was unusual was that she only called Sundays and Thursdays and it was Wednesday.

"Chris, I'd like your opinion on the prayer-chain," said Helen. "My son Jim joined yesterday and for some reason it feels important to me where I place him in the calling order. I assumed Dorothy would call him since she and Jim know each other well, but my gut says it should be you."

My tears had started flowing the moment I realized that Jim Gerbracht — a man who'd just buried his five-year-old daughter – had joined the prayer chain and was willing to pray for other people's issues or illnesses. It was probably the purest act of Grace I'd ever encountered. Then, before I could fully process the gift of Jim's courage and maturity, Helen mentioned her gut instinct that I should be the person to call Jim! It was all too much, this flood of grace and love, and my heart and soul couldn't process it.

"Bettina predicted this!" I managed to say to Helen through my tears. "Carole made a way for it to happen!" and I told her the whole story of Carole's visitations and how resistant I'd been about being her messenger. Not only had Carole made it possible for me to talk with her father, she'd provided Jim and me additional common ground to start the conversation on.

I even had 24 hours to prepare for the call, but I discovered that rather than make pre-call notes, I just savored the entire order of events that preceded the call. For me, this was one giant miracle that spread itself out over three days.

As it turns out, there was even more grace coming. The next evening, after Helen phoned with a few new names for the prayer list, I called Jim to give him the entire list, which had maybe 50 entries. When the "business" of the call had been concluded, I told Jim about how impressed I was by his joining the prayer-chain group at all. He said he thought it would probably help with his mourning and that all prayer had a healing quality for him.

The time had come. I took a huge breath to bolster my courage.

"Jim," I started, "I want to share something with you that lots of people would say is crazy, or impossible, or both."

Jim jumped right in to reassure me. "Whatever it is, I can guarantee that won't be my reaction."

"Okay, well, here goes. I actually believe that Carole's spirit came to me in a dream and commanded me to give you a message to deliver to Adele. Carole said, 'Tell my dad to tell my mom that I am holding her in arms of love.'"

"Oh, that definitely was Carole!" said Jim instantly and just as instantly, I was completely at ease. This opened a floodgate of words that had been piling up.

"I told Carole I didn't think it was my job to deliver her message, but she wasn't having it. It's like her soul isn't five years old, but is as old and wise as a prophet instead. Oh, and she said she loved you and Adele equally, but her 'concern' for Adele was greater at this time. And she said that I would give you this message even as I tried to assure her that I NEVER would — and that all messages given in love are perfectly timed. And it must be true, at least for her, since she timed her visits with me on the night before and the night after you joined the phone prayer chain!"

Jim probably heard how needlessly I was rushing through the whole story and again broke in to reassure me. "Thank you!" he said. "There is absolutely no doubt in my mind that you heard from Carole."

I'd done it, just like Carole had said I would, and judging from Jim's reaction, it was a perfectly timed message of love from Carole to Jim and Adele – and me! In two brief dreams, Carole had taught me more about truth than anyone else ever.

"Jim, now that I've delivered Carole's message, I have a question for you. How have you dealt with all your anger? The angriest I've ever been in my life was the evening Carole died! I can't even imagine how much anger you must be processing."

"It's strange that you ask," said Jim, "because Adele and I were just talking about that. In all the days since Carole died, I've never felt anger or resentment toward God, even though I expected I would. Who knows, maybe you processed all of my anger for me."

Even twenty years later, I'm still moved by Jim's generosity of spirit. Talk about the fruit not falling far from the tree! Jim was as God-centered as his mother Helen, and his daughter Carole was such an advanced soul that she could orchestrate miraculous happenings on earth from her place in heaven. I can't say for sure if what Jim suggested — that one person can process another's anger for them — is even possible, but I knew absolutely that I was being blessed beyond all measure by every member of the Gerbracht family. That Jim could even consider that all my self-centered, fear-driven rage following Carole's death could be a favor to him, could only come from divine imagination.

The phrase "the message is love" popped back into my head. There had been countless love messages to me that I hadn't realized were loving and holy. I also hadn't appreciated the fact that whether they were from Helen, Carole, Claudia, Pat, Bettina, or now, Jim, they had all been perfectly timed.

"Jim, I'm feeling so blessed and grateful — by you, your mom and Carole – that I feel like I need to get off the phone to go say thank you to God for like an hour straight."

We hung up and I took the prayer-chain list with me out the door, the same list that began with "The Gerbracht Family, Jim, Adele, Claudia and Carole."

As I walked, a full moon popped out from above the clouds that were perched above the Australian pines at the end of my street. And I pledged to the moon and its Creator that from now on, my job would be to share all the messages of love I ever encountered — and, God willing, the timing would always be perfect.

Postscript:

When a friend of ours in Key West said we could house-sit her home for a few weeks in January 2000, we jumped all over the offer. When we'd moved away from Key West five months earlier for me to begin seminary, we'd sold our duplex and now were in that 98% of humanity who couldn't afford to vacation there, at least not during the three weeks of winter vacation when Key West was jammed with super-moneyed folk from all over the northern hemisphere!

We were all grateful to be back – Bettina, our daughters who were now 9 and 3, and me. We all loved things about our old hometown. Within an hour of arriving, I passed on taking a walk around Old Town, preferring instead to do my traditional drive around the island and get far enough away from Old Town to buy less expensive groceries at the new Publix store. Key West isn't big, being a peanut-shaped island about three miles long, so in no time at all, I'd driven by our old house, the Peace Covenant Presbyterian Church where the Key West Pre-School Co-op was located, and the house where a drug dealer lived with the meanest dog on the planet. On the spur of the moment, I decided to finish my circumnavigation of the island in the direction that would get me to Publix five minutes later, but give me an "open-sea" view of the ocean rather than the boat and island-filled view from what we locals called "the Gulf-side." Driving down Atlantic Boulevard, less than a minute from the ocean, I saw a man in the distance step out of a minivan and open the sliding door to the back seats.

As I got closer, I realized it was Jim Gerbracht, parked in front of their home, the same address where his five-year-old Carole had died two years earlier.

Although I hadn't thought about the Gerbrachts for a while, I had heard through the grapevine that they had been considering adopting a 12-year-old from Russia named Kristina. Besides her name and that she was small for her age, I hadn't heard anything more, including whether or not they had succeeded in finalizing the adoption.

Just as I remembered that, and in the same fraction of a second where I had the most advantageous location to see it, Jim reached into the minivan and a blond-haired girl, the same size as Carole was when she died, jumped off the seat and into Jim's arms, her arms encircling his neck tightly at the precise moment I was closest to their driveway. If I had driven down the street ten seconds earlier or later, I would have missed her jump as well as the hugging arms of love between father and daughter.

Less than a minute later, I was driving along Smathers Beach looking over the same water that Claudia Gerbracht had looked over when she spotted her sister in the clouds. "I love you," Carole had said that night, and truer words had never been spoken.

Overprotective

I've always been overprotective, but I haven't always known it. And when I learned that I was, I didn't know why.

Apparently, this character flaw got a lot worse when I became a father. When Maya was born in December of 1990, it's as if my capacity to truly love was born with her. Better men would have already known more about love than I did, men who were better sons, brothers, friends, and especially husbands than I was, but fatherhood awoke a new, powerful all-encompassing love that I'd never felt before. As crazy as it might sound, the only thing that was even vaguely similar to my love for my baby daughter was the love I had always felt for music. But in Maya, the beauty and transcendence I'd sensed in music was now flesh. Being Maya's father was now my highest calling and my reason to be — my solitary goal was to nurture and protect her. And, unknowingly, over-protect her.

Almost immediately, I had opportunities to see that I was both over-parenting and over-protecting, but I deflected or denied them all. When my wife, Bettina, and I brought Maya home from her first visit to the pediatrician, Bettina mentioned to me how she had sneaked a glance at the doctor's private chart and seen that he'd made a note that said "Parents overprotective?" Although I had liked the doctor and been impressed by his calm demeanor (a quality I lacked then), I went straight on the defensive. "There's no such thing as overprotective," I announced. "He probably neglected his own children and is threatened by really nurturing parents. I had two parents just like him!"

I'm sure Bettina noticed the huge amount of falsehood and foolishness in my response, but she also knew me well enough to know when I wasn't open to a topic, so she let it go. Bettina understood that there was a positive side to my overprotectiveness as well; because I could do almost everything our hand-painted clothing business required with Maya right on my chest inside a Guatemalan papoose, Maya and I were inseparable. In fact, at the laundry/café run by Cuban ex-pats where Maya and I logged long hours heat-setting painted shirts and washing her cloth diapers, one shy woman got a translator to ask me a question: "Does your baby have a mother?"

When I think back to the 1990s, the entire decade is a blur of doing the same tasks, non-stop, 18 hours a day. I was a dad, a businessman, and a housekeeper, but everything I did had a single obsessive focus: being the protector and provider for my daughter, and, after Sophia was born in May of 1996, my daughters. It may have been a blur, but the over-arching philosophy of "nurture and protect" was a simple and good one, no matter how compulsive I was about it. Life was very good, all in all.

Sure there were lots of diapers, but I now had a new Maytag and I'd hang them on a huge clothesline next to countless T-shirts, tank tops and sweatshirts painted with Bettina's happy designs in primary-color fabric paint.

When I was taking care of the girls, I was also able to blend in lots of other work tasks, and this was especially true as Maya grew into a very nurturing (much) older sister. Her care for her little sister exceeded what every parent hoped a sibling could manage. While I would make a phone call to a sweatshirt wholesaler while feeding mushed avocado and banana to Sophia, Maya would make feeding her sister a single task; Sophia would get the same food, but with undistracted love. I'd frequently hear Maya explaining something to Sophia, or giving her instructions, using the identical words or phrases I'd said to her five years earlier. But while Maya said the same things, there would be a calm loving-ness to her that I'd never gotten exactly right. Said another way, Maya was sane in ways I'd been neurotic, and appropriately protective where I was overprotective.

That gap in psychological and behavioral health was never more apparent than it was on November 27, 1998, and the months that followed. It was Black Friday, the day after Thanksgiving, but for those of us who worked in industries that were tourist-driven, it was pretty much a day of working rather than shopping. Because Bettina and I had had stronger than expected sales through Thanksgiving Day, we needed to crank out more product than we'd planned so we'd be perfectly stocked for the remainder of the weekend. To maximize productivity, I'd dropped Bettina, our girls and Maya's friend Ashley off at a cute little county park called Astroland, and returned the mile home to work exclusively on shirt production.

Within ten minutes of arriving home, however, I had the strangest – and strongest — intuition that I should return to the park. "I am returning to the park two hours from now, like Bettina and I planned," I internally dialogued with my intuition. My intuition firmly countered with, "Don't stay here longer than 3-5 minutes!" and the power of the command wouldn't have been stronger if it had been shouted from an officer in the Marine Corps.

I grabbed my keys, hopped in the station wagon and immediately wondered how I would explain my early return to Astroland. I wasn't worried about Bettina's reaction, because she had witnessed my intuition's accuracy on more than one occasion. For example, when I'd known Bettina for less than an hour, I told her we would marry and have a blond-haired blue-eyed daughter — which, in addition to being insane-sounding, was a genetic long-shot since Bettina has dark brown hair and hazel eyes. We both knew that my hunches were often accurate, even if we didn't understand how they worked or where they came from. I was just as baffled about the strength and forcefulness of this intuition as I knew Bettina would be by my early return to the park.

The two of us never did have that discussion about intuition, however, because within seconds of my getting there, Maya climbed off the parallel bars and jogged over to me. "Dad, do you see that man with the grey shirt?" she calmly asked, and pointed to a man just beginning to cross the street, "There must be a hole in that man's pants because his penis was hanging out.

And he was shaking it at me and Ashley with a weird look on his face."

I was already headed to the gate, "Get Ashley and stay with your mom," I barked, "and call the police!" I caught up with The Flasher across the street, grabbed him by his T-shirt collar and pulled him back from the doorway of the public restroom before he could sneak in and hide. "Listen, asshole," I hissed into his right ear, "you and I are gonna stand right here until the cops come" – and in an instant, he broke my hold on him, spun and took off down the sand and coral of County Beach. The chase was on.

An interesting thing I've learned about these super-adrenaline moments is that they are often accompanied by what feels like total calm. One is completely in the moment and time slows to non-existence. In that slowest super-slow motion, I remember calmly wondering, as I was chasing him, if The Flasher had broken the ring finger on my right hand when he broke my grasp on his T-shirt. I remember about a minute into the chase observing his short muscular legs sprinting along the beach and estimating whether he was getting ahead of me or if we were going the same speed. I deducted that he was going just slightly faster than I was. I yelled as I ran, "Stop that man," and I remember seeing one college-age kid's face as he considered whether he would get involved or not as well as his "can't help you, bro'" look as I ran by him.

In addition to being slow-motion, it was also like I was watching the whole thing on TV. Although it was me chasing The Flasher, it actually felt more like watching a live news report of someone I knew who was chasing some deviant, but I wasn't involved or at risk.

If there was one way it wasn't like a news report, though, it's that there was no wide angle shot or helicopter overview or I would have seen the police car coming up on our side with flashing lights and no siren. The officer pulled directly in front of The Flasher and ordered us both to stop.

    It took a while to sort things out. First, the officer thought I was the "bad guy" chasing someone innocent and I was so out of breath at first (I had raging high blood pressure at the time) I literally could not speak in my defense. Second, after I eventually explained the problem, the officer astonishingly replied, "Well, if he didn't actually touch the girls, there's been no crime." At that point, my daddy-bear instincts kicked in and I began to act like Billy Martin getting into an umpire's face at Yankee Stadium. "Get on that radio and get another officer here and MAKE SURE it's an officer with daughters!" I commanded, and praise God, he did what I asked without Tasing me.

    Another officer arrived quickly after the first officer's request and I actually started interrogating him. "Are you a father?" (a nod yes) and "Any daughters?" I demanded, and the second he said, "Yes, a girl and a boy," his tone and body language said that he was in charge now, thank you, and the job interview was over. "We'll take care of everything," he said and I believed he would. I felt myself immediately converting back to a calm human from a rabid bear. It's amazing how quickly everyone can be calmed down when a capable person who embodies a "non-anxious presence" is injected into a chaotic situation. In less than ten minutes after the "take charge" officer arrived, The Flasher had been arrested, handcuffed, and charged with a double felony (Lewd and Lascivious Behavior / Assault of a Minor Child). It might have been because of his treatment by the same wise and competent officer, but it seemed as if even The Flasher felt calmer, almost relieved, when they put the cuffs on him.

    I was calm, too, or at least calmer, until I learned at the police station that The Flasher, Darrell Ray, had raped a seven-year-old girl in Alabama five years earlier and that his sentence had been entirely suspended (meaning he hadn't gone to prison for a day)! The police also shared that he had another felony conviction and that his actions today would be his "third strike," which was a Bill Clinton-era term in which felonious triple offenders got huge prison sentences. But at this point, I was only half-listening, because after I heard about the rape in Alabama and pictured Darrell several feet from my own seven-year-old exposing himself, I decided I was going to kill him. Not metaphorically, but actually. Kill him dead, and at the earliest possible opportunity.

    In retrospect, the scariest thing about my plan was how absolutely serious I was about it. When I shared it with the police, they assured me that I'd feel different after a night's sleep, but I didn't really sleep that night. Instead, I tossed around in bed planning how I could best assassinate Darrell. What would ensure the perfect fatal-yet-merciful headshot as they took him from the city jail to the preliminary trial, I wondered, having never owned a gun in my life? I dozed a little bit, I guess, but when I did, I dreamed I was beating Darrell and screaming things at him that were so vicious, graphic and gruesome that I was surprised at myself even in the dream.

Fortunately, God sent an angel, and sent one fast. Not that I recognized that the prosecuting attorney was an angel at the time, but I did realize it decades later. His first gift to me was to remain calm and respectful when I was completely agitated and irrational. When I straight-facedly shared my plan (which was four days old and getting detailed) to shoot Darrell, he met me where I was by saying, "I totally understand your feelings because I feel the same way sometimes, but please do me a favor and let me prosecute him for his felonies and not you for manslaughter!" As a people-pleaser, I fell for this strategy immediately. By not shooting Darrell, I would be doing this guy a favor! Then he doubled down. "That's what's best for me and Monroe County and it's also what's best for Maya. You protect her best when you let us take care of Darrell."

This guy had mad skills! He had completely disarmed the murderous ticking bomb that I'd become. And as if that weren't enough positive persuasion, he then talked me into seeing a therapist (something I'd probably needed my entire life, but never done) with the same bit of sales genius that he'd used to get me to give up my plans to murder Darrell Ray — it would help others! "Chris," he said to me like we were the two best fathers on earth, "did you know that when a minor is a victim of a crime, then legally, every member of the entire family is the victim of the crime?" I pondered this; it felt right. He continued. "Monroe County is right to cover the cost of a therapist not only for Maya, but for the whole family. You or your wife could go too, together or alone, to speak with a counselor about how best to support your daughters now."

He knew he'd made the sale but put some whipped cream on. "You'll want to be as supportive of Maya as possible, since we're expecting her to testify at the trial — that girl's a pistol!"

Mad skills!! In less than a quarter hour, I'd been talked out of committing a murder and convinced to start the work necessary to figure out where all the anger fueling that bad idea was coming from. And I realized — again, years later — that the prosecuting attorney had clearly known the entire time that I was the only one in the family that needed a shrink.

And I was the only one who went. They say God is good, but that's probably an understatement. My therapist, Dr. Good, was certainly proof that God was great! And just like the prosecuting attorney, he gained my trust by affirming how important it was to do the work of getting in touch with everything the "incident" had stirred up. Before we were half an hour into the first session, Dr. Good started focusing on the strength of my reaction to Darrell Ray. Over eight sessions, the only questions he asked, besides basic information (Are you married? Does Maya have siblings? Seen a psychotherapist before?), were always centered on the degree of anger and violence I felt toward Darrell Ray and why did I think I felt it so strongly?
Again, with hindsight, I realized that Dr. Good very likely knew the answer to his own question, but it wasn't going to be of any value to me unless I figured out the answer myself. Which I didn't in my sessions with him, although dancing around the truth did much to calm me down and give me perspective.

And I kept a lid on my diminished anger through the next months and was mostly rational through Darrell's trial (which included Maya's calm and detailed testimony), his conviction and final sentencing – 15 years in a Florida penitentiary.

And with that concluded, I stopped seeing Dr. Good. He was kind and encouraging in the final session and seemed especially pleased to hear that I'd been accepted into a seminary where seeing a psychotherapist was required during the first year.

It was during that time in seminary that I discovered that I had also been so "overprotective" of some of the details of my own early years that I had repressed them completely from conscious memory. Although it may have helped me to ignore a huge part of my own story for almost forty years, I believe that God wanted me to face all the truths of my life, and to face them in God's good, actually great, time.

++++++++++++++++++++++++++++++

Postscript:

In 2002, while crossing Brattle St. in Cambridge, Massachusetts, in a part of town where people are usually staid and exceptionally well-behaved, a car crossed directly in front of my daughters and me while we were in the crosswalk. In one extended motion, I grabbed my six-year-old, Sophia, back from the car with my left hand and kicked the car so hard with my right foot that the dent stretched from the back left wheel well to the bumper. The driver stopped and looked back and when his window started to lower I raged through the crack, "Get out of that car, asshole, and it'll be the last stupid thing you ever do!"

    As he drove off, I turned to my daughters and realized that I'd probably traumatized them as much as the driver of the freshly dented Acura, and maybe more. In an instant, I thought of my spiritual director (something like a God-believing psychotherapist) who was a monk at the monastery around the corner, and how I'd likely confess my extreme over-reaction and hyper-vigilance to him. I thought of the weekly therapy group I attended — Victims of Violence: Survivors of Childhood Sexual Abuse — and pictured myself sharing the same story. Still hyperventilating from the adrenaline, I panted to myself, "I am here…now. I'm a work in progress, I'm moving from shame to Grace."

    Then to my daughters I said, "Girls, that was a giant over-reaction on my part and I apologize to you both. Situations like that are very difficult for me to get right." Maya, now eleven, instantly countered,

"No, Dad, you did the right thing — he really was close to Sophia and it was scary!" And she took my hand — she was already holding Sophia's hand with the other — and marched us safely to the seminary cafeteria.

Meeting Mister President

In 2011, I quit a job I was good at and walked away from a $150,000-a-year salary. Predictably, no one thought this was a good idea, and what made it extra difficult for most people was the fact that what I wanted to do next seemed unlikely to produce an income any time soon — or maybe ever — since what I'd decided to do was write a movie.

Adding to the insanity of my decision was the fact that the thing I hated most in the world was writing. In high school, college and grad school, I would put off writing papers until the night before they were due, and then allot one page per hour counting back from when the paper was due. For example, if a 10-page paper were due at 9 a.m., I would delay the start of the actual writing until 11 o'clock the night before, write one page per hour during my "all-nighter," turn it in punctually in the morning and then come home for a long nap.

Looking back, it's not surprising that I didn't spend much time writing after I quit my job. Unlike college and grad school, there were no deadlines.

I could make all the notes I wanted and dream up ever catchier movie plots, but nothing ever forced me to finish a single script. And I didn't.

So a true and accurate inventory of my shortcomings would have included that I was a procrastinator or just plain lazy, but I had additional writer's flaws as well. In fact, the procrastination and sloth were symptoms of a bigger underlying problem that can only be described as karmic generational blockage. My father had published eight or nine books while teaching at seminary, and the possibility of writing something that didn't connect or succeed made me especially nervous since I would be failing at something in which he had excelled. And to complete the perfect storm of writer's block, I add the neurosis of my perfectionism and the final affliction of the worst case of ADHD in the history of the world.

In retrospect, the wisest thing might've been to not buy Final Draft (a screenwriting software program), but instead get a battery of good therapists to coax me through the karmic landmine of my flaws and fears. Truthfully, though, even if I'd done all that, I probably would have continued to make writing a way lower priority than living. After working non-stop from the age of 8 to 52, the idea of catching up on my sleep, playtime, exercise and traveling appealed to my healthy side and my lazy side both.

One fun thing I'd been too busy to do several years earlier was something that my wife and daughters had done without me and loved. While living in Jesup, Georgia, they'd driven to another small town, Plains, to attend a weekly Bible class that was taught by

Jimmy Carter at a small Baptist church. Yes, the former president and Nobel Prize winner actually taught an hour-long Bible class most Sundays of the year, although he still traveled the world as a diplomatic adviser and humanitarian. Because I worked every Sunday morning as a pastor at my own church, I stayed in Jesup and only enjoyed their visit vicariously. Even that was pretty significant, however, because they returned home with an adorable photo of Jimmy and Roslyn Carter smiling like proud and loving grandparents with their hands gently holding my daughters' shoulders.

In the six years since my family's visit to Plains, we'd left Georgia for Florida where I began the job that I would quit four years later. Whether I was now on an "unpaid sabbatical" (my preferred description) or was instead just an unemployed and aimless wanderer is hard to say. Regardless, I was on a multi-stop road trip that included time with my older daughter in Tallahassee and the ordination of a friend in Savannah. But the new and adventurous part of the trip was going to Plains, where I'd never been, and seeing Jimmy Carter, whom I'd never seen.

I confess I was super-excited as I waited for Jimmy to enter the sanctuary to begin his Bible class; it felt like everyone in the room was excited, and it was contagious. I was also a little bit nervous because before Jimmy came into the sanctuary, a woman who was a member of the church came out to let us know ALL the rules. She was half master of ceremonies who wanted us to feel warmly welcomed to the church and half Marine drill sergeant who prepped us on etiquette, particularly on what NOT to do when Jimmy was present. I would have needed a notebook for all the rules and recommendations, but I realized I would be able to avoid over half the pitfalls if I just pledged to never speak a syllable. Then I would not have to worry about committing the common gaffe of referring to Jimmy's wife as "Rahs-lyn" instead of the correct pronunciation, "Rose-lynn." I wouldn't make the mistake of addressing Mr. Carter as "Mister President," which everyone should know refers solely to the sitting president! "So unless Barack Obama walks in that door in a few minutes, the address 'Mister President' should not be heard this morning!" said our rule-giver.

  She spoke at length about not speaking at length. "Jimmy invariably asks people where they are from, but please don't insult him or the rest of the group by saying Chicago, Illinois, when Chicago is sufficient. Or Illinois, but we don't need both." I promised myself I would not ask Jimmy Carter a question on any topic, theological or geo-political, even if I were BURNING for his insight on a matter. I would be a fly on the wall, listen, learn and leave. My vow of silence began now and under no condition would I say a word all morning to President Carter or anyone else!

  But it turned out there was a bigger sin than long-windedness that was also to be avoided at the Maranatha Baptist Church; touching the president or Mrs. Carter during the photo-taking time after the service was forbidden by the Secret Service, a prohibition that the rule-giver especially applauded since "shaking a million hands is nothing an 87-year-old needs to be doing. When you approach the president, do NOT extend your hand for a handshake; get your photo taken as quickly as possible and we can get the Carters off to a timely lunch," she said. "That's just good manners!" I had lived in the South long enough to know the extra weight given to good manners, so to "don't talk" I added "don't touch" — which would be easy since flies on walls don't do either.

At exactly 9:30 a.m., Jimmy walked into the church to huge applause that he instantly quieted with practiced power and perfect modesty. What happened next, I can only blame on my clothing; in the interest of honoring the church and Jimmy, I'd worn my best and most formal clerical clothes. Imagine if a clergy collar and suit had a tuxedo equivalent and that's what I was wearing. Furthermore, because I had a certain type of clergy collar (a "tab" collar), most people would have assumed that I was probably a Roman Catholic, rather than Episcopal, priest. The moment Jimmy had quieted the applause, he looked straight at me and said, "Welcome Father, thank you for joining us." "Thanks for having me," I said quickly, wondering if my answer could have been shorter or whether I should have added a "sir." Jimmy was still looking right at me and only at me. "Where are you from?" he asked, and I said with unnecessary speed "Florida" and made a mental calculation how many fewer syllables Florida was (3) than St. Petersburg (4), or — worst option — St. Petersburg, Florida (7)! "Florida," Jimmy said in that slow Georgia voice, probably to let everyone know that we could relax and say things at their normal length and speed. "Well, it's wonderful to have you here!"

On one level, the man is so familiar that you feel as comfortable as you would with an old friend, but on another level, even then, I did think to myself, "Good God, a president of the United States AND a Nobel Peace

Prize winner just welcomed me to his Bible class." And more amazing than that, Jimmy, as a life-long Baptist positively would have known the Bible verse that says, "Do not call anyone on earth 'father,' for you have one Father, and he is in heaven" (MT 23:9). That same man just called me FATHER with warmth and pure welcome. Talk about creating a mood!

The president continued with that welcoming tone and asked several other people where they were from, sometimes asking follow-up questions as well. Then Jimmy invited all clergy — ministers, pastors and missionaries — to stand. About 25-30 of us did, all but one of whom was male. Without a moment's pause, Jimmy asked the one woman standing if she would begin our Bible study with prayer. She did and knocked it out of the park — one of those true "God speakers" who speaks straight to God with reverence yet familiarity. The enthusiastic 350-person "amen" at the end of her prayer showed that everyone agreed; she'd inspired us and set a Godly and loving tone for the study hour.

As for the actual Bible study, I truthfully don't remember a single detail because the specifics were dwarfed by the much bigger theme of Jimmy's inclusivity and loving humanitarian tone. I may not remember the questions he was asked, but I will never forget the careful and caring response that every single question received.

When the Bible study ended, I thought to myself that everything was so perfect, I didn't need more from the morning. I would have jumped in my car and skipped the regular church service if I hadn't planned to wait for the photo opportunity after the service when Jimmy and Roslyn allowed all the photo taking. I thought it would be fun to have a matching photo to go along with the photo of the family — minus me — from six years earlier.

Still, the earliest that photo could take place was going to be at least an hour and a half from now, since a half-hour break had just begun and then the service would be another hour, minimum. I hatched a new plan as only a guy who'd spent a million hours at church could hatch. I'd sneak down to a coffee shop in town, eat breakfast and read the paper to pass the time before returning to the church to get my photo with the Carters. A quick trip to the men's room and I'd be on my way. I purposefully avoided the main social hall and its bigger, newer bathroom because I didn't want anyone to notice that I was sneaking off.

There's an old expression, "If you want to make God laugh, tell God your plans!" My plans to drive to town and blow off church were less than a minute old when, while I was using one of two urinals in the tiny church men's room that was off an old hallway, Jimmy walked in and appeared at my shoulder to use the vacant one. "Hello again, Father," he said and I blundered back, "Hello, Mister President."

If Jimmy bothered to notice that I'd just addressed Barack Obama, he didn't let it show on his face. Jimmy spoke like he'd been expecting to run into me. "I hope it was okay with you that I asked the woman to lead the opening prayer," he said, with genuine concern that I might maybe have felt slighted. "Better than okay," I said. "I thought it was the perfect choice since she could not have prayed a better prayer. That was pure Holy Spirit!" I gushed. Jimmy paused, a long time, like he was re-living the prayer and said finally, "Yes, I agree with you."

While Jimmy said a few extra words about how important it was to "normalize female leadership in the church," my mind was racing, in spite of my casual demeanor. Were either of the two Secret Service agents going to walk in to check on their "protectee?" And if they let Jimmy go to the men's room unaccompanied, should I imitate them and let him have a moment of quiet solitude, and exit the bathroom this second?

By now I'd finished washing my hands and left the water running for him. "I'm going to say goodbye this second and leave," I thought, when Jimmy asked, "So where in Florida is your parish?" OH MY GOD!!! PLEASE DON'T TELL ME JIMMY REMEMBERED THAT!! And I was the first person, of many, that he had talked to that morning. I was impressed but truthfully, also a pinch embarrassed to admit that I'd been inactive as a priest for a year and a half, but I went with the unvarnished truth. "My last parish was in St. Petersburg," I said, "but lately I've been living half there and half in California learning how to write screenplays." Jimmy made a warm thoughtful sound, halfway between "ahh" and "ohh," turned to face me directly, looked me straight in the eye and said, "So you are a writer now." We both knew he had just made a pronouncement; I had received an affirming executive order, but it felt like the executive was God and Jimmy was the angel-messenger.

After drying his hands, Jimmy picked up the book he had set on top of the hand dryer when he'd first entered and said, "I've written as well. This is my latest project," and modestly, actually hesitantly, he held out his new book. At first glance, I saw a picture of a beautiful field at sunset and saw the words "Lessons From Life."

Jimmy opened it and I realized it was actually a Bible that had a lifetime's worth of notes and reflections interspersed with the text. But this finished project was also his working Bible; although he had just published it, this copy had a few fresh ink entries next to his printed commentary — a work forever in progress.

I felt like it was my turn to say something, but I was stuck looking at the fresh scribbles in the Gospel of Luke. I swear Jimmy sensed that I was getting ready to say something gushy and dumb about his dedication to Bible study, so he continued, "I've done a few things with Zondervan, the publishers; they're really very good people to work with." Did Jimmy know that I had, for about the tenth time that morning, noticed how naturally and effortlessly he lives the characteristic of Christian modesty? You cannot fake it — at least not with me, you can't. I'd been a priest long enough to sort out the genuine from the phony.

Our conversation was easily at the 10-12 minute point, making it the longest conversation, by far, that I had ever had in a men's room with anyone. The Secret Service men had never even stuck their heads in the door. Right about then, I had this intuition that however long this conversation was going to be, Jimmy was not going to signal or initiate the end of it. When neither of us had said anything for a moment, it's like I knew he would have stood there all day in humble silence waiting for me to say something as a wrap-up. Rather than say, "President Carter, what a great honor it's been ... blah blah blah ...," I simply said, "I think it might be about time for us to praise and thank God," and I ceremoniously took a step toward the bathroom door.

He paused and again looked straight at me and I felt like the pure love of God was flowing directly to me through the conduit of his gaze. "Yes, I guess it is that time," said Jimmy, and then added slowly, "I've enjoyed our conversation — and I look forward to reading your work!"

He reached out an old wise hand, the one that I'd promised not to shake, and I took it, no longer worried about breaking all the rules.

Before becoming an author, Chris Schuller had a number of careers, from being a rock n' roll singer to working as an ordained priest in Episcopal churches. Chris lives in Los Angeles.

For additional copies or more information about this book go to crazygodstuff.com or email the author at pastorchrislove@gmail.com.

Made in the USA
Middletown, DE
16 March 2019